1001 CIVIL WAR TRIVIA

By Charles B. O'Brien

Charles B. O'Brien

NEIRBO BOOKS

First Edition 1991: Heritage Books, Inc.
ISBN 1-55613-424-X

Second Edition 1994: Neirbo Books.
ISBN 0-9637602-0-3

Gilbert White discovered the formula for complete happiness, but he died before making the announcement, leaving it for me to do so. It is to be very busy with the unimportant.

Edward Newton

PREFACE

As a member of A. P. Hill Camp, Sons of Confederate Veterans, I felt a need to stimulate interest for members in the interesting and informative facts concerning the American Civil War. So I started offering to the members of the organization a small monetary award to the member who presented the most correct answers to a number of trivia questions given to them at a previous meeting. Both Union and Confederate questions were used. After compiling the questions a number of times, I got the idea to compile a large number of questions and look for a publisher.

The second publisher I contacted liked the idea and especially liked the fact that all answers were reliably documented. To further authenticate my sources, I verified them with Allan Nevins' Civil War Books-- A Critical Bibliography. If the review was not favorable, the source was not used.

Author

INTRODUCTION

This book covers only one category--the American Civil War. It contains a thousand and one questions and answers of amazing facts and sensational truths of the Civil War. With this book, you have in front of you a collection of facts that will enable you to amaze and astonish your family and friends--even yourself. Though the questions may at times seem difficult, what's difficult for one person may be a cinch for the next. It is hoped that the questions and answers will be interesting to the point that the reader will further pursue his or her interest in the war--or pursue <u>new</u> areas of interest. <u>A starting point for the reader is the provided documentation for each answer, including page number</u> (You won't see this in other trivia books).

Some seeming errors may probably be the differences of opinions of authors. For example, questions concerning the "beginning of the war" may be open to opinion because there was not an official declaration of war by either side. Therefore, consensus of experts and general knowledge have been used.

QUESTIONS

1. Name the last southern state to secede.

2. In what theatre was Lincoln assassinated?

3. Who was known as Ol' Bory?

4. Who said, "It is well war is so terrible, or we should get too fond of it"?

5. How old was Scarlett O'Hara at the beginning of *Gone With the Wind*?

6. From what city did Sherman begin his march to the sea?

7. When Lee retreated toward Appomattox, whose army was he trying to join?

8. Who was called the Hero of Sumter?

9. Who played the part of Rhett Butler in *Gone With the Wind*?

10. What was General Joseph Hooker's nickname?

11. Union soldiers ate a staple bread. What was it called?

12. In what battle was the bloodiest day of the war?

13. What woman was hanged for her alleged role in Lincoln's assassination?

14. Name the only recorded civilian casualty at the Battle of Gettysburg.

15. Who took the first photograph from a balloon?

16. Up to March, 1862, what naval battle was the first of its kind?

17. How many people attended the theatre with Lincoln on the night of his assassination?

18. Who preceded Abraham Lincoln as U.S. president?

19. What was the home state of General Winfield Scott?

20. Who gave Stonewall Jackson his nickname?

21. What was Stonewall Jackson's only military defeat?

Stonewall Jackson

22. From what state was Union General George Thomas?

23. Who were the Copperheads?

24. What Civil War nurse established the American Red Cross?

25. What Union cavalry general was killed by Sioux Indians after the war?

26. What do the initials G.A.R. stand for?

27. What did Robert E. Lee call artillerist John Pelham?

28. What was the Thirteenth Amendment?

29. In *Gone With the Wind*, what was the name of the O'Hara home?

30. Who was known as the Fighting Bishop?

31. Who was the most famous drummer boy?

32. What was the Sibley tent?

33. Who wrote the "Battle Hymn of the Republic"?

34. Name the first Union commander of occupying forces in New Orleans.

35. What was the first major army commanded by Lee?

36. Which side won the Seven Days Campaign?

37. Who was Confederate commander at Second Manassas (Bull Run)?

38. In what state was the Battle of Antietam fought?

39. Who was Union commander at the Battle of Fredericksburg?

40. Who assumed command of Stonewall Jackson's troops after he was wounded?

41. Who won the Battle of the *Monitor* and *Merrimac* (*Virginia*)?

The *Monitor* and the *Merrimac*

42. Name the most famous Confederate woman spy.

43. What river did the Union army cross to attack at Fredericksburg?

44. What speaker preceded Lincoln at Gettysburg?

45. What engagement became known as the Battle Above the Clouds?

46. What Union general was "corked in a bottle" by Beauregard?

47. Who replaced Johnston as commander of the Army of Tennessee against Sherman in 1864?

48. Name Lincoln's second-term vice-presidential candidate.

49. Who commanded the C.S.S. *Alabama*?

50. Where did Admiral Farragut say, "Damn the torpedoes! Full speed ahead"?

51. Who was Union commander at the Battle of Nashville?

52. Name the last Confederate port to remain partially open.

53. What famous president rode over Fort Stedman, Petersburg after the battle that took place there?

54. What two armies were involved in the war's last *major* engagement?

55. Where was the last *major* engagement of the war?

56. Where did Lee hold his final council?

57. To whom did Confederate General Joseph Johnston surrender his army?

58. Which side won the last significant land battle of the war?

59. In whose barn were John Wilkes Booth and his accomplice found?

60. What country furnished the most foreign-born soldiers?

61. Whose last words were, "Strike the tent"?

62. What southern state was the first to secede?

63. Who was general-in-chief of the U.S. Army at the beginning of the war?

64. What company completed the first transcontinental telegraph?

65. Where was Union General McDowell's headquarters at First Bull Run?

66. Who was McClellan's chief of secret service?

67. Who was Rose O'Neal Greenhow?

68. Who was Union superintendent of nurses?

69. Who was Union commander at Second Bull Run?

70. Where was the greatest cavalry battle fought on American soil?

71. Name the dates of the Battle of Gettysburg.

72. Who was Union commander at Vicksburg?

73. Who wrote the song "Dixie"?

74. Who was Edwin Stanton's chief detective?

75. How many black soldiers earned the Congressional Medal of Honor during the besieging of Petersburg, Virginia in 1864?

76. What Confederate general was known as Ol' Pete?

77. How did Lincoln's assassin break his leg?

78. Who was Lee's "right arm"?

79. What battle is famous for Little Round Top, the Wheat Field, Peach Orchard, and Devil's Den?

80. What general said, "War is hell"?

81. In what battle was Confederate General A.S. Johnston mortally wounded?

82. Who was Union naval commander at the Battle of New Orleans?

83. Name the date of the surrender at Vicksburg.

84. Who was Union commander at Shiloh?

85. Who won the Battle of Fredericksburg?

86. Who was Confederate commander of the famous ride around McClellan?

87. Two Union soldiers found a paper wrapped around three cigars. What was the paper?

88. Where was the Bloody Angle?

89. Who was Lincoln's opponent in the 1864 presidential election?

90. Who said, "Let us cross over the river and rest under the shade of the trees"?

91. What Union general wrote *Ben Hur*?

92. Who was Confederate commander at the Battle of Winchester?

93. What was the Lost Order of Antietam?

94. Who was called the Rock of Chickamauga?

95. What Union general took Atlanta?

96. Who assassinated Lincoln?

97. What famous Civil War song was played at Jefferson Davis's inauguration?

98. Who was first offered command of the Union army?

99. Who built the Federal ironclad *Monitor*?

100. Who shot Stonewall Jackson at Chancellorsville?

101. How did the Union ironclad *Monitor* end its career?

102. What battle is considered by Civil War authorities as Lee's greatest?

103. Who succeeded Burnside as commander of the Army of the Potomac?

104. What famous action ended the Battle of Gettysburg?

105. In what battle did VMI cadets take part?

106. In what battle was Jeb Stuart mortally wounded?

107. Who replaced Hooker as commander of the Army of the Potomac?

108. What was the popular name of Confederate prison Camp Sumter?

109. What was the original name of the Confederate ironclad C.S.S. *Virginia*?

110. Who was Union commander at Gettysburg?

111. What was Grant's first major battle against Lee?

112. What year did Lee become general-in-chief of the Armies of the Confederacy?

113. Who said, "I propose to fight it out on this line if it takes all summer"?

114. What Union general had a policy of allowing "camp followers" into soldiers' bivouacs?

Robert E. Lee

115. What city was considered second in importance only to Richmond?

116. At whose home did Lee surrender to Grant?

117. What was Lincoln's assassin's profession?

118. Which arm of Stonewall Jackson's was amputated?

119. Which leg did Lincoln's assassin injure?

120. Name Jeb Stuart's chief of artillery.

121. Who treated Lincoln's assassin's injured leg?

122. Why were there often two names for the same battle?

123. In *Gone With the Wind*, what was the family name of the twins who courted Scarlett O'Hara?

124. Name Jeb Stuart's favorite musician.

125. What was the Civil War soldier's most important item of equipment?

126. What general was known as Beast?

127. Name at least nine of the seceded states.

128. At Bull Run a general shouted, "Look! There is Jackson standing like a stone wall!" State his next four words.

129. What was inscribed in all records of martial history as the grandest charge?

130. What was the Petersburg Crater?

131. In *Gone With the Wind*, with whom was Scarlett O'Hara in love?

132. Name the elongated bullet of soft lead, about one inch long, pointed at one end and hollowed out at the base.

133. Where was Jefferson Davis imprisoned after the war?

134. Where was Lincoln carried after he was shot?

135. How many states comprised the Confederacy?

136. What was known by all soldiers as graybacks?

137. In 1861, how many chaplains were allowed in each regiment of the Union Army?

138. In rank, what was the Union naval equivalent of a brigadier general?

139. Name the Confederate general who surrendered to General U.S. Grant at Vicksburg.

140. How long did the siege of Petersburg last?

141. Which U.S. military service assaulted John Brown at Harper's Ferry?

142. What Confederate general's name was on the lips of both Lee and Jackson as they lay dying?

143. In what type of building was John Brown cornered at Harper's Ferry?

144. Of what religion was Robert E. Lee?

145. What was the major railroad city in Virginia?

146. Who was known as Little Mac?

147. Name the Union general known as the Young Napoleon.

148. Who was known as Prince John?

149. Of what religion was Judah P. Benjamin, Confederate secretary of war?

150. Who led the VMI cadets at the Battle of New Market?

151. Who was Lincoln's first vice-president?

152. Who led the U.S. troops in the capture of John Brown?

153. At what battle was Burnside's Bridge?

154. Of what religion was P.G.T. Beauregard?

155. At what battle was the Dunker Church?

156. In *Gone With the Wind*, what was Scarlett O'Hara's first name?

157. What U.S. Army rank did Robert E. Lee hold at the time of John Brown's raid at Harper's Ferry?

158. Who carried the surrender demand to John Brown at Harper's Ferry?

159. Who wrote *Gone With the Wind*?

160. Of what religion was General Leonidas Polk?

161. Who wrote *Lee's Lieutenants*?

162. Name the quartermaster general of the Union Army.

163. Who followed Andrew Johnson as president of the United States?

164. What office did Robert E. Lee hold after the war?

165. Name the most prominent Negro statesman during the Civil War.

166. In what state was Fort Pillow located?

167. Who was president of the United States during the Civil War?

168. When was *Gone With the Wind* released as a motion picture?

169. At what battle did Grant break Lee's line to capture Petersburg?

170. Who was president of the Confederacy during the Civil War?

171. What constitutional amendment freed the slaves?

172. What was Confederate General Thomas Jackson's most popular nickname?

173. What was the name of Robert E. Lee's most famous horse?

174. Name the commander of the Union armies at the end of the war.

175. Who was Hannibal Hamlin?

176. Name Robert E. Lee's cavalry chief.

177. What Union general made the famous march through Georgia?

178. Name the commander of the Confederate armies at the end of the war.

179. In what state did Lincoln make his famous Gettysburg Address?

180. Name the second capital of the Confederacy.

181. Where did Lee surrender to Grant?

182. What is the popular name of the famous charge at Gettysburg?

183. What famous military students fought at the Battle of New Market?

184. Who was the most famous Civil War photographer?

185. Who replaced Stonewall Jackson as commander of the Stonewall Brigade?

186. Who wrote *Uncle Tom's Cabin?*

187. In what state was the (in)famous Andersonville prison?

188. Who was Robert E. Lee's father?

189. Where was Libby Prison?

190. Who directed the movie *The Birth of a Nation?*

191. Who played the role of Ashley Wilkes in *Gone With the Wind?*

192. What was Lincoln's profession before being elected president?

193. What was the name of Harriet Beecher Stowe's famous novel?

194. What Union general captured Atlanta?

195. Who was Andrew Johnson?

196. In what city is Lincoln buried?

Abraham Lincoln

197. In *Gone With the Wind*, what was the name of Ashley Wilkes's home?

198. What actress played the role of Melanie Hamilton in *Gone With the Wind*?

199. Why were Union Generals James Ledlie and Edward Ferrera censured after the Battle of the Crater at Petersburg, Virginia?

200. Where is former President of the U.S. and former Confederate John Tyler buried?

201. Who remarked, "I don't see how we could have an army without music"?

202. What town in Vermont was "captured" by the Confederates?

203. From what state did troops say as a rallying cry, "First at Bethel, farthest at Gettysburg, last at Appomattox"?

204. A replica of the house in which Lee and Grant signed surrender terms was dedicated to a National Park in 1950. Descendants of two famous generals were present. Who were they?

205. Who was the first person in history to place an order for machine guns?

206. Of what nationality or descendancy were most army bands?

207. To whom were Virginia Military Institute cadets referring when they said, "Dead on the Field of Honor, Sir"?

208. One town in Virginia changed hands 76 times during the war. Name the town.

209. What happened to Confederate General Joseph E. Johnston at Union General Wm. T. Sherman's burial?

210. How many words are in the Gettysburg Address?

211. What was the name of the only American submarine to sink an enemy vessel?

212. Who was the only admiral/general in the Confederacy?

213. What civilian is known as the Hero of Gettysburg?

214. What was the motto on the Confederate States of America Great Seal?

215. Name the basic weapon (brand) used by the infantry soldier.

216. Who said the U.S. Civil War was "the last great war fought by gentlemen"?

217. What was the date of the Battle of the *Monitor* and *Virginia* (*Merrimac*)?

218. What Confederate general was also known as Tom Fool and Old Blue Light?

219. Where is Marye's Heights?

220. On what day of the week was the Battle of the *Monitor* and the *Virginia* (*Merrimac*)?

221. In the Union army, how did the enlisted soldier wear his haversack?

222. Why was Lincoln's youngest son, Thomas, called Tad?

223. What was the name of Lincoln's presidential steamship?

224. Who, in earlier years, had obtained a West Point cadetship for Confederate General George Pickett?

225. What rank did Lincoln's son, Robert, hold in the army in 1865?

226. Who said, "There has been no such army since the days of Julius Caesar"?

227. Name the star of the play Lincoln attended when he was assassinated.

228. Who was the second president to be assassinated?

229. Who was head pallbearer at Lincoln's funeral?

230. In what city is John Wilkes Booth buried?

231. Of what type of wood was Lincoln's coffin?

232. What was known as Black Easter?

233. Who invented the minie ball?

234. In what city was John Brown hanged?

235. What facial hair was named after a Union general?

236. Who was Confederate commander at the battle of Nashville?

237. The most famous of Lee's horses was Traveller. Name two of his other mounts.

238. Name Stonewall Jackson's chief mapmaker.

239. What was the date of Lincoln's assassination?

240. Where was the last temporary Confederate capital?

241. Who was the Confederacy's last postmaster general?

242. What Union unit had the largest number of killed or mortally wounded in any one engagement?

243. Who was medical director of Stonewall Jackson's Corps?

244. When a Union soldier was at the pay table, who usually waited at the table with him?

245. In what part of the day did Lee surrender to Grant?

246. Name the first capital of the Confederacy.

247. In 1862 the *Atlantic Monthly* printed a poem which was to become a famous song. Name the song.

248. What was the full name of Lincoln's son Willie?

249. Name three of the five full Confederate generals appointed in 1861.

250. Name the only Indian Confederate general.

251. What Union general, because of his temper, was nicknamed Old Snapping Turtle?

252. Name Stonewall Jackson's horse.

253. Who led the Union party that stole a southern locomotive in Georgia?

254. Hornet's Nest, Bloody Pond, Peach Orchard, and Sunken Road are associated with what battle?

255. How did the Confederates lose the C.S.S *Virginia* (*Merrimac*)?

256. Name Stonewall Jackson's cavalry chief.

257. Where did Stonewall Jackson die?

258. What Union cavalry commander attempted a raid on Richmond in March 1864?

259. Why has one of several photographs taken of Lincoln in February, 1864 become famous?

260. Grant held the highest rank in the U.S. Army since George Washington. What was that rank?

Ulysses S. Grant

261. Where was the most sensational prison escape of the war?

262. What was Confederate General W.B. Jones's nickname?

263. Lincoln came under fire when he visited Fort Stevens, D.C. Who told him, "Get down, you fool"?

264. When did the Thirteenth Amendment officially become a part of the Constitution?

265. Who commanded the Union fleet at the first attack on Fort Fisher, North Carolina?

266. What city was the ultimate goal for Sherman after Savannah?

267. What state was the first to ratify the Thirteenth Amendment?

268. Why was a certain battle nicknamed the Battle of Kilpatrick's Pants?

269. To whose home was Lincoln carried after his assassination?

270. In what town was Jefferson Davis captured?

271. The southern soldier ate "coosh." What is coosh?

272. Where was Jefferson Davis inaugurated as President of the Confederacy?

273. What Union commander captured Fort Hatteras, North Carolina in 1861?

274. Whose nickname was Fuss and Feathers?

275. What was a "Quaker Gun"?

276. On which side did poet Sidney Lanier serve?

277. Name the last battle in Stonewall Jackson's Shenandoah Valley campaign.

278. What new naval force was used by Confederates in Charleston, South Carolina in 1863?

279. Who invented the Confederate submarine C.S.S. *H.L. Hunley?*

280. Name the date of Lincoln's Gettysburg Address.

281. Who wrote "The Bivouac of the Dead"?

282. Where was Union General George Meade born?

283. How many sons did Lincoln have?

284. What famous Italian patriot and soldier was offered a generalship in the Union army?

285. What Union general had the honor of receiving the surrender of Lee's army?

286. What battle proved that a water approach to Richmond by the Federals was impractical?

287. How old was Robert E. Lee at the beginning of the war?

288. Within 100 pounds, an average of how many pounds of lead were needed to hit an enemy soldier?

289. Why was each Union army enrollee's teeth closely examined by surgeons?

290. What Union general wore whiskers that formed the letter "W" on his upper lip and jowls?

291. Where did McClellan's army retreat to after the Seven Days Campaign?

292. What Confederate general escaped from Ohio State Penitentiary?

293. Who said, "I have come to you from the west, where we have always seen the backs of our enemies"?

294. What incident ended McClellan's military career?

295. Who commanded the Union Negro 1st South Carolina Volunteer Infantry?

296. What was the purpose of Kilpatrick's Raid on Richmond?

297. What percent of the Confederate armies were foreign-born?

298. What was General Nathan F. Evans's nickname?

299. Name Lincoln's personal secretary.

300. What was Burnside's second attempt to cross the Rappahannock River near Fredericksburg, Virginia called?

301. Of what religion was Stonewall Jackson?

302. What was the longest sustained operation of the war?

303. On what day did Lee surrender the Army of Northern Virginia?

304. Who stabbed Secretary of State William Seward?

305. How many brothers-in-law did Lincoln have serving in the Confederate Army?

306. What was the name of the play Lincoln attended the night of his assassination?

307. Which side won the Battle of Missionary Ridge?

308. Which ex-president of the United States was elected to the Confederate States Congress?

309. What was Jefferson Davis doing when he received news of the disaster to Lee's army?

310. What military action cut off Wilmington, North Carolina as a blockade-running port?

311. Who was President Lincoln's bodyguard?

312. What was the last major Confederate city to fall?

313. How was the C.S.S. *Albemarle* sunk at Plymouth, North Carolina?

314. What two armies fought the Battle of Nashville?

315. Where was the *intended* Confederate concentration point after evacuating Petersburg and Richmond?

316. Where were the Lincoln conspirators hanged?

317. What year was the first national income tax passed?

318. How many Union sutlers were allowed per field regiment by Army regulations?

319. On what charge was the commander of Andersonville prison convicted?

320. Where was John Wilkes Booth first buried?

321. What owner/editor had as a masthead on the *New York Tribune* the words "Forward to Richmond"?

322. What famous message did General Sherman send to Lincoln on December 22, 1864?

323. To what city did President Jefferson Davis go after the evacuation of Richmond?

324. After whom did Jeb Stuart name his daughter?

325. Name the last Confederate garrison on the Mississippi River to surrender.

326. Who was Confederate commander at the Battle of New Market, Virginia?

327. What rank did Winfield Scott hold in the U.S. Army?

328. Name the largest battle fought in Missouri.

Rifle pits

329. Where was Confederate General Nathan Bedford Forrest born?

330. Who was Confederate commander at Vicksburg?

331. Who was with John Wilkes Booth during his escape?

332. Where was the first balloon ascension made from a Federal vessel?

333. Who commanded the last Confederate attack on Fort Stedman, at Petersburg, Virginia?

334. Who is credited with shooting John Wilkes Booth?

John Wilkes Booth

335. What incident was described by a New York newspaper as "the great tragedy of our age"?

336. Who was senior Confederate general at the beginning of the war?

337. Where was the greatest naval bombardment of the war?

338. Name Lincoln's four sons.

339. In the movie *Gone With the Wind*, who played the part of Jonas Wilkerson?

340. According to General James Longstreet, what was General George Pickett's greatest battle?

341. What was the name of Union Captain Farragut's flagship?

342. To whom was the Lost Order of Antietam addressed?

343. How tall was Robert E. Lee?

344. The railroad raid in Georgia was referred to as the "great locomotive chase." Name the stolen locomotive.

345. What was the Dictator?

346. Name one of the two men who entered the Petersburg Crater tunnel and relit the fuse.

347. Who were General William T. Sherman's "bummers"?

348. Name the Union commander at Chickamauga.

349. How many roll calls were made daily in the Union Army?

350. When Union posts were established, who named them?

351. What was the short-waisted, single-breasted jacket worn by Confederates called?

352. Who was "Lieutenant Harry T. Buford"?

353. How many men were with John Brown at his raid on Harper's Ferry?

354. Name at least two roll calls made in the Union Army.

355. What was the nickname for Fort Sedgewick in Petersburg, Virginia?

356. Where was Fort Darling?

357. Who was Elizabeth Van Lew?

358. What was the name of General U.S. Grant's horse?

359. What was the nickname for Fort Mahone in Petersburg, Virginia?

360. Who commanded the United States Sharpshooters?

361. Name the Confederate Secretary of the Navy.

362. What town saw more marching armies than any other?

363. Name the "railroad genius" of the Union Army.

364. What is a "gabion"?

365. Where was the greatest supply base of the war located?

366. Who wrote the original order of Robert E. Lee's Farewell Address?

367. Who led the first Union attack on Petersburg in 1864?

368. What battle was the war's bloodiest two-day fight?

369. What famous essayist, humorist, and short story writer served with Ninth Indiana Division?

370. What famous World War II general's father served with the 24th Wisconsin Division in the Civil War?

371. Who was the Union's first "martyr"?

372. What infantry manual was most widely used by both sides?

373. Name the basic artillery weapon used in the war.

374. Who saved Little Round Top for the Union at the Battle of Gettysburg?

375. What family owned the farmhouse that General Meade used as headquarters at Gettysburg?

376. Where were the first Confederate forts to surrender?

377. Where was the first naval engagement in the war?

378. Where was the first skirmish in the war?

379. Who wrote *A Diary From Dixie*?

380. Who was Jefferson Davis's physician during his imprisonment?

381. Who set the official prices a sutler could charge for his wares?

382. What state did the first Negro to sit in the Congress of the United States after the war represent?

383. What Confederate state was the last to be re-admitted to the Union after the war?

384. Who first commanded the Irish Brigade?

385. What Confederate state had the largest number of free Negroes at the beginning of the war?

386. What was General William T. Sherman's wife's first name?

387. Who was the first full admiral in American history?

388. What former high office did the Confederate secretary of war hold?

389. Of what nationality was the commandant of Andersonville prison?

390. What were latrines, or toilets, called during the war?

391. Where was the southernmost point of the Union blockade?

392. Under what circumstances were Union soldiers served whiskey?

393. Name the first hospital ship of the U.S. Navy.

394. Of what religion was General A.P. Hill?

395. What member of Lincoln's cabinet did not attend his funeral?

396. How many people were hanged for Lincoln's assassination?

397. Of what religion was President Jefferson Davis?

398. Why was one member of Lincoln's cabinet missing at his funeral?

399. To what prison were some of the Lincoln conspirators assigned?

400. Of what religion was General James Longstreet?

401. Name Stonewall Jackson's favorite fruit.

402. Name three of the four great rivers that separated the Union and Confederate capitals.

403. In the Union army draft, what was the most widespread cause for exemption?

404. Who was Confederate commander at the Battle of Nashville?

405. What Confederate general set up his own makeshift naval/cavalry command?

406. Who was Governor of Georgia in 1864?

407. What was the biggest battle west of the Mississippi?

408. What was a more popular name for New Madrid Bend on the Mississippi?

409. How long after his election in 1860 did Lincoln sign a bill ending slavery in the District of Columbia?

410. Who was personally in charge of digging the Union tunnel at Petersburg, Virginia?

411. Name the courier who was with General A.P. Hill when he was killed.

412. Where was the first field tent hospital established?

413. Name the Confederate commander in the New Mexico Territory in 1862.

414. Which army won the Battle of Pea Ridge, Arkansas?

415. Name the first Negro regiment sent from the North.

416. What were the age limits of the Confederate Conscription Act of April, 1862?

417. Who was with Lee at the McLean house when he surrendered?

418. What was the average height of the Union soldier?

419. To the nearest thousand, approximately how many military actions or "fights" occurred during the Civil War?

420. What was Jefferson Davis doing when he was informed of his election as Confederate president?

421. What was the only known fatality of the first shelling of Fort Sumter?

422. In essence, what was the Crittenden Resolution passed by the U.S. Congress in 1861?

423. What war aid did the King of Siam offer President Lincoln?

424. What was the pay of Union army nurses in 1861?

425. Who was president of the U.S. Sanitary Commission?

426. How old was Lincoln's assassin?

427. Name the ex-sutler's clerk who later became a well-known circus owner.

428. Who did Carl Sandburg call "the most shot-at man in the war"?

429. For which side did Henry Stanley of "Dr. Livingston, I presume" fame serve?

430. Who was Confederate commander at the Battle of Pea Ridge, Arkansas?

431. Why did Lincoln rescind a Union general's orders that all slaves in certain areas were declared free?

432. What general succeeded General Joseph Johnston when he was wounded at the battle of Seven Pines?

Hospital at Fair Oaks (Seven Pines)

433. Who was Union commander at the Battle of Winchester?

434. Who was second-in-command of Confederate forces at Shiloh?

435. Name the last Confederate ironclad to operate in the Mississippi River.

436. What was unique about the First Regiment, Louisiana Native Guards (Union)?

437. For whom did Robert Yeadon offer a $10,000 reward--dead or alive?

438. Who was Confederate commander at the Battle of Murfreesboro?

439. Against whom was General Grant's controversial General Order No. 11?

440. What was the Swamp Angel?

441. Name the Confederate commander at the Battle of Chickamauga.

442. What president had a son die during the war?

443. What words did the victor use to inform Lincoln his army had taken Atlanta, Georgia?

444. Name the Union commander at the Battle of New Market, Virginia.

445. Why, in 1864, was Lincoln insisting that as many soldiers as possible be allowed to go home?

446. Name two of the three commanders who conferred with Lincoln at City Point, Virginia, in March 1865.

447. How many vessels were required for Lincoln to get to Richmond after its evacuation?

448. What was the height of the shortest man in the Union army?

449. What was the main provision of the first national income tax?

450. Which state is the only one that has ever had two of its sons serve as President *at the same time?*

451. At the Battle of First Bull Run, how many bullets (within 1000) has it been estimated were fired for every man killed or wounded?

452. What were the *Laird Rams?*

453. What was the average age of enlisted men in the Union army?

454. Who invented the breech-loading machine gun used by the Confederates at the Battle of Seven Pines?

455. Name one of Union General Phil Sheridan's horses.

456. Who was the first soldier in the Army of the Potomac to be executed?

457. Name three of the various commanders of the Confederate Army of Tennessee.

458. What was the weather in Washington, D.C. on Election Day, 1864?

459. What was the salary range of drafted Union surgeons?

460. Who made the first successful vessel-transported balloon reconnaissance?

461. Who was Union commander at the Battle of Pea Ridge, Arkansas?

462. Where was the first naval battle fought with Japan?

463. What is the *official* date of the end of the war?

464. What military position did Jefferson Davis hold before being elected president of the Confederacy?

465. What oath did the citizens of Chincoteague Island, Virginia take in 1861?

466. What was the name of General McClellan's horse at the beginning of the war?

467. What was the average weight of the Union soldier?

468. What was General William T. Sherman's job before the war?

469. Who led the largest escape from Libby prison in Richmond, Virginia?

470. What was General McClellan's wife's first name?

471. Name the major battle fought in Florida.

472. Where were the Federals "bottled up" by General Beauregard?

473. Jefferson Davis once pulled money from his pocket and threw it to a crowd. Why?

474. What did General McClellan's head of Secret Service do before the war?

475. What event was referred to as "Colonel Rose's tunnel"?

476. Where did the Union army cross the James River in its move from Cold Harbor, Virginia to Petersburg, Virginia?

477. In which White House room did the body of Lincoln lie in state?

478. What was the name of the vessel that was the first to transport a balloon for observation purposes?

479. Where did the U.S.S. *Kearsage* sink the C.S.S. *Alabama*?

480. What Union general commanded the occupation of Richmond?

481. How old was Abraham Lincoln when he was assassinated?

482. Whose granddaughter unfurled the first Confederate flag at Montgomery, Alabama?

483. Name Lincoln's Negro barber.

484. What Union regiment was mobbed by Baltimore ruffians while on their way to Washington, D.C.?

Fort Sumter

485. How did Confederate General Philip St. George Cocke die?

486. Who preached Lincoln's funeral sermon?

487. Who was Mother Bickerdyke?

488. What was the height of the tallest man in the Union army?

489. What military service was most represented in Lincoln's escort as he entered the Confederate White House?

490. What event caused the Confederate government to cease to exist?

491. What were the main items of the last meal served in Fort Sumter, South Carolina before its surrender?

492. Name the Negro headwaiter at Washington's Willard Hotel Restaurant.

493. Who wrote and issued the famous *unauthorized* emancipation proclamation?

494. Name two of the three Confederate generals assigned to arrange the details of Lee's surrender to Grant.

495. When Confederate General George Pickett said, "Keep up a Skookum tum-tum," what did he mean?

496. What state was the second to secede from the Union?

497. Where was General P.G.T. Beauregard born?

498. Who was the first doctor to minister to Lincoln after he was shot?

499. Who was the first military balloonist to serve with American troops?

500. What was the first vessel to be *specially designed* as an aircraft carrier?

501. How much did Robert E. Lee weigh at the beginning of the war?

502. On the day Lincoln was assassinated, what time did the fatal shooting take place?

503. How old was the doctor who first ministered to Lincoln after he was shot?

504. How much money did the Union allow to clothe a private soldier for one year?

505. For how long did a sutler hold office?

506. Name one of the two framed prints on the wall of the room where Lincoln died.

507. How often were Union soldiers mustered for pay?

508. What was the Union reward for apprehension and delivery of a deserter?

509. A famous authoress called Robert E. Lee a "weak man." Who was she?

510. How much per month was deducted from Union enlisted soldiers to support the Soldier's Home?

511. Within five dollars, what was the monthly pay of a Union infantry private?

512. Name the first commander-in-chief of the United Confederate Veterans.

513. Who was the first president of the Southern Historical Society?

514. In what year did the biggest of all Confederate reunions take place?

515. Within five dollars, what was the monthly pay of a Union brigadier general?

516. When a Union enlisted soldier lost a Colt revolver, how much was he charged?

517. Name the judge who sentenced John Brown to hang.

518. Name Stonewall Jackson's chaplain.

519. Within five dollars, what was the monthly pay of a Union sergeant major?

520. How many musicians were allowed per Union brigade in volunteer service?

521. What was the sutler's limit of legal claim upon a Union officer or enlisted man?

522. How many laundresses were allowed per company in the Union army?

523. Who served as General Robert E. Lee's cook during the war?

524. Who pioneered the anti-personnel mine?

525. Name the oldest corps leader of the war.

526. Who commanded the Tramp Brigade?

527. Who was known as Scrappy Billy?

528. Who commanded General Sherman's XIV Corps in the march to the sea?

General Sherman

529. Who was first assistant engineer of the U.S.S. *Monitor*?

530. Who was the youngest Confederate general?

531. Name Stonewall Jackson's wartime cook.

532. What was the name of the first ship in history to be sunk by a submarine?

533. Who commanded the Union division that attacked at the Battle of the Crater in Petersburg, Virginia?

534. Who was General Grant's military secretary?

535. Who was the first Confederate general to be captured on the field at the Battle of Gettysburg?

536. Who commanded the Union Negro Division at the Battle of the Crater?

537. Who ordered the destruction of Virginia Military Institute (VMI) after the Battle of New Market?

538. How was Confederate General Earl Van Dorn killed?

539. By 1860, approximately how many photographers were plying the trade? (Answer must be within 400).

540. What was the main reason that there were very few Confederate sutlers?

541. In July, 1864, at Petersburg, Virginia, General George Pickett asked General Lee for a pass to visit Richmond. Why did Pickett want this pass?

542. Name the first Confederate general killed in the Civil War.

543. Where was the first monument to commemorate the Civil War erected?

544. What act marked the commencement of the Civil War?

545. Name the first Union soldier killed by enemy action.

546. In what year was Virginia re-admitted to the Union?

547. Name the first naval chaplain killed in action.

548. Name the first Negro to sit in the Congress of the United States.

549. Name the first Confederate *officer* killed in the Civil War.

550. Name the U.S. District judge who presided over Jefferson Davis's trial in 1867.

551. What was Virginia known as before its re-admission to the Union?

552. What prominent Northern editor was the first to sign the bail bond for Jefferson Davis?

553. What Union general appointed himself as a Mississippi senator?

554. Young boys and Negroes called them "Jeff Davis's musical boxes." What were they?

555. Name the date Richmond, Virginia fell.

556. What was the first aircraft carrier?

Jefferson Davis

557. Of what religion was General Nathan Bedford Forrest?

558. What famous future Confederate was considered for nomination for U.S. president by the future Union General Benjamin Butler?

559. Who was the first Negro Union army officer?

560. In what unique manner was Lincoln's Amnesty Proclamation delivered behind the Confederate lines?

561. What event precipitated General D.H. Hill's promotion to brigadier general, C.S.A.?

562. Who was responsible for Lincoln's beard?

563. Who was the first known machine gunner?

564. Name the youngest general officer in the Civil War.

565. How old was Ulysses S. Grant in 1861?

566. How much was the author paid for the poem "The Battle Hymn of the Republic"?

567. Whose sword did John Brown brandish during his raid on Harper's Ferry?

568. Name the youngest Confederate general officer.

569. Name three of the four future members of the Supreme Court who fought for the Union.

570. The 8th Wisconsin Regiment had a unique mascot. What was it?

571. Within five, how many horses did Confederate General Nathan Bedford Forrest have shot from under him?

572. Name two of the three future members of the Supreme Court who fought for the Confederacy.

573. Name the last surviving lieutenant general of the Confederacy.

574. Within 50, how many nuns served as battlefield nurses?

575. Name the female spy to whom General Jeb Stuart gave a commission.

A 13-inch mortar

576. Where was the Confederate Navy Yard located after the fall of Norfolk and Portsmouth, Virginia?

577. How did a famous Confederate spy convey a message to General Beauregard before the Battle of Bull Run?

578. Up to the end of the war, where was the largest hospital ever built in the Western hemisphere?

579. What was the name of the first Union submarine?

580. Who said, "The only unfailing friend the Confederacy ever had was cornfield peas"?

581. Which member of the Committee on the Conduct of the War had previous military experience or military education?

582. Who was the last man to see Lincoln's face?

583. Within 20, how many funeral marches were written for Lincoln in 1865?

584. What town in Pennsylvania was ordered by the Confederates to pay half a million dollars ransom?

585. Who commanded the U.S.S. *Monitor* at the end of the battle with the C.S.S. *Virginia* (*Merrimac*)?

586. Within five, how many times were the coffined remains of Lincoln moved from one place to another?

587. Who was in command of the C.S.S. *Virginia* (*Merrimac*) at the end of the battle with the U.S.S. *Monitor*?

588. What was used to carry Lincoln to a lodging house after he was shot?

589. Who said about Lincoln, "Now he belongs to the ages"?

590. Who received the reward for capturing John Wilkes Booth?

591. What group comprised Lincoln's pallbearers?

592. To whom was President Andrew Johnson referring when he said, "She kept the nest where the egg was hatched"?

The house in which Lincoln died

593. At what hour did Lincoln die?

594. Name the hangman at Lincoln's conspirator's hanging.

595. What was the name of the riderless horse behind Lincoln's last funeral parade?

596. What was the name of the engine that pulled Lincoln's funeral train from Washington, D.C. to New York?

597. Who was the chief witness against Mary Surratt at her Lincoln conspiracy trial?

598. What was the name of the engine that pulled Lincoln's funeral train from New York?

599. In the movie *Gone With the Wind*, what are the last words spoken?

600. Within 10,000, how many Negroes joined the Union forces?

601. Who was wartime governor of Virginia?

602. What was the capital of Georgia during the Civil War?

603. Who led the conspiracy to assassinate Lincoln on his way to be inaugurated in Washington, D.C?

604. What annoying habit did Union General Henry Halleck have?

605. Name two of Jeb Stuart's famous scouts.

606. Who did Secretary of War Edwin Stanton believe to be the mastermind of the plot to assassinate Lincoln?

607. What was President Andrew Johnson's former trade?

608. What Union general invented a breech-loading carbine?

609. What Catholic chaplain of the Irish Brigade later became president of Notre Dame?

610. What Union general undertook the largest amphibious operation in the western world?

611. How many men did General Jeb Stuart lose in his famous ride around the Union army?

612. What was the largest army Robert E. Lee ever commanded in the field?

613. In *Gone with the Wind*, what was the last name of Miss (Aunt) Pittypat?

614. What was the Bohemian Brigade?

615. What general said, "McClellan knows I am a better general than he ever dared hope to be"?

616. For how long had General George Meade been commander of the Army of the Potomac before the Battle of Gettysburg?

617. What was the perennial theme song of the Army of the Potomac?

618. What was the South's most important crop?

619. What was the subtitle of *Uncle Tom's Cabin*?

620. How many Southern states had seceded by the time Fort Sumter, South Carolina fell?

621. What famous wealthy man was on General George McClellan's staff?

622. How many drummers did each Union infantry company have?

623. How did Union General McClellan take Yorktown, Virginia?

624. What battle was named after two different kinds of trees?

Lincoln in Gen. McClellan's tent

625. Who was Confederate second-in-command at the Battle of Gettysburg?

626. How old was General George Pickett when he made his famous charge?

627. How did General Stonewall Jackson rank in his West Point graduation?

628. Which Confederate general, because of his physical appearance, was sometimes mistaken for General Robert E. Lee?

629. What two Confederate states' troops did not participate in Pickett's charge at Gettysburg?

630. How many graduates were in the West Point class of 1846?

631. What color was Union General William T. Sherman's hair?

632. What was meant when soldiers said, "Well, Bill has turned up his toes to the daisies"?

633. What was Union General William T. Sherman's opinion of slavery before the war?

634. What date did Richmond fall?

635. Who was the Confederate chief of ordnance?

636. Where did the Union general who commanded the occupation of Richmond make his headquarters?

637. About whom was South Carolina's influential James Henry Hammond speaking when he said, "He is as vain as a peacock, as ambitious as the devil"?

638. What happened to Elizabeth Van Lew (Crazy Bet) after the war?

639. How was a Union regiment entitled to call itself a Veteran Volunteer Regiment?

640. Which side had more trouble with desertions?

641. What was Ulysses S. Grant's original name?

642. What Union general was known as Old Brains?

643. What changed the maxim: "The best defense is a good offense"?

644. How many sons did General Lee have in the Southern army?

645. How much was paid for the table where Lee sat at the surrender at Appomattox?

646. What interim cabinet post did General U.S. Grant hold after the war?

647. Who was governor of Pennsylvania when Lincoln made his Gettysburg Address?

648. What woman served as nurse, spy, and soldier for the Union?

649. What nurse was called Mother?

650. What was the name of Jefferson Davis's plantation?

651. Why were there thirteen (13) stars in the Confederate flag?

652. Who headed the Confederate Department of Agriculture?

653. Of what denomination was the first Confederate postage stamp?

654. How many secretaries of war did the Confederacy have during the war?

655. What one important European nation was hostile to the Confederacy?

656. What Confederate general held the post of superintendent of the U.S. Military Academy for only five days?

657. Who was the first general officer on either side to be killed in action?

658. Where was General U.S. Grant when Lincoln was assassinated?

659. What general initiated the equivalent of today's U.S. Army shoulder patch?

660. According to old-army procedure, how was "taps" given?

661. In the Union army, how long were the first volunteers enlisted for?

662. What Kentucky senator had one son a Confederate general and one son a Union general?

663. What trick was used to keep mules from braying at night?

664. What were known as Beecher's Bibles?

665. What was the fundamental fighting unit of both armies?

666. What was the Stonewall Brigade initially known as?

667. What Union admiral had two sons in the Confederate army?

668. In his farewell speech to the First Brigade (Stonewall Brigade), how did Stonewall Jackson refer to the Civil War?

669. After a reconnoiter near Winchester, Virginia, why was Confederate Captain John O'Brien the first member of a staff to return to his unit?

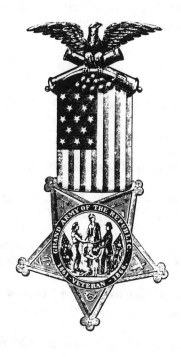

670. Approximately how many men were in the U.S. Army in 1861?

671. How many U.S. ships were captured by the Confederacy at Norfolk, Virginia?

672. What is the approximate total of men who served in the Union army?

673. How did the North name its armies?

674. What battle was often called the Bull Run of the West?

675. What event caused the Committee on the Conduct of the War to be formed?

676. What were the chances of surviving a wound in the Civil War?

677. What Union cavalry commander wrote a five-act military drama entitled *Allatoona*?

678. Who was known as the aeronaut of the Army of the Potomac?

679. What was Stonewall Jackson's first wife's name?

680. Who was Heros Von Borcke?

681. Who was governor of Massachusetts during the war?

682. Who first commanded the 54th Massachusetts Volunteer Regiment (Negro)?

683. What famous Negro leader had two sons in the 54th Massachusetts Volunteer Regiment (Negro)?

684. Within 10,000, how many free Negroes were in the Confederacy?

685. What was the name of President Jefferson Davis's coachman?

686. Where were slaves first introduced into the English colonies?

687. Who commanded the C.S.S. *Virginia* (*Merrimac*) in its first engagement?

688. How many hostile shots did Mark Twain, the famous author, fire during the war?

689. How many separate motions had to be made to fire a Civil War musket?

690. How many future presidents of the United States served as officers in the Union army?

691. Where is the largest Civil War cemetery?

692. What prison had the highest death rate of all Civil War prisons?

693. In which state occurred the largest number of engagements?

694. What was the Confederacy's first invasion of the North?

695. Name the church that figured prominently at the Battle of Antietam.

696. What famous nurse was at the Battle of Antietam?

697. At Confederate Andersonville prison, who were the Raiders?

698. What was the largest division in the Confederate armies?

699. Where is General A.P. Hill buried?

700. What was the name of the creek that ran through Andersonville prison?

701. How were Federal Corps numbered?

702. Who was probably the youngest Confederate soldier?

703. What Federal regiment consisted of all Germans?

704. What Confederate general was the last to surrender his troops?

705. To what item was the Union soldier referring when he said, "ferry-boats," "tanyards," or "pontoons"?

706. What was the Confiscation Act?

707. What did the Southern soldier refer to as a "she-bang"?

708. How long was the typical bayonet?

709. What was the average marching speed?

710. What did the soldier do when he "foraged"?

711. Name one of the most popular pictorial newspapers read in Union army camps.

712. Why, by 1864, was the Army of the James frequently called the Army of the Games?

713. What was the most popular spare-time occupation of Civil War soldiers?

714. How many physicians did the Confederate armies have?

715. What was the first and most prevalent offense committed by both Union and Confederate armies?

716. What was the salary of a Union chaplain?

717. What building stands on the site where the commandant of Andersonville was hanged?

718. Before battle, what was the usual allotment of ammunition per man?

719. What was a "red badge of courage"?

720. Who was the first general in American history to command an army of 30,000 men?

721. By what name did many officers address General Ambrose Burnside?

722. To what Union general was Lincoln referring when he said, "I am his friend because nobody else is"?

723. What was Union General McClellan's opinion of Lincoln's Emancipation Proclamation?

General McClellan

724. When Lincoln relieved General McClellan of command, what one word describes his reason?

725. How old was General Grant when he was appointed general-in-chief of the Northern armies?

726. Why did the Confederacy not have a Supreme court?

727. How many members were in the Confederate First Congress?

728. How many secretaries of state did Jefferson Davis have?

729. Which president commuted every death sentence for desertion that came across his desk?

730. Name the largest of all Confederate war industries.

731. What were "shinplasters"?

732. What was the original name of West Virginia after seceding from Virginia?

733. After Sherman's march to the sea, how many states had portions remaining in Confederate control?

734. What was the Confederate 20-Negro Draft Exemption Law?

735. Which Confederate high official was blind in one eye?

736. During the siege of Vicksburg, why did shelling of the city cease at 8:00 AM, Noon, and 8:00 PM?

Grant's headquarters at Vicksburg

737. Under what kind of tree did the two commanders meet for surrender negotiations at Vicksburg?

738. What was the motto of the 22nd Regiment, U.S. Colored Troops?

739. What is the motto of the State of Virginia?

740. What was the highest rank attained by blacks during the war?

741. How many VMI cadets participated in the Battle of New Market?

742. By what name did his troops affectionately call General William T. Sherman?

743. Who wrote the song "Marching Through Georgia"?

744. Who organized the Confederacy's first spy ring?

745. What unit was known as the "marchingest" regiment in the Union army?

746. How many children did General William T. Sherman have?

747. What was General U.S. Grant's first Civil War command?

748. What proclamation did President Andrew Johnson issue concerning President Jefferson Davis?

749. For a time after his swearing-in as President, why did Andrew Johnson not have an office?

750. After his capture, where was Jefferson Davis first taken?

751. After whom is Howard University in Washington, D.C. named?

752. What gift of sympathy did Pope Pious IX send to Jefferson Davis?

753. What color did General Robert E. Lee describe his horse Traveller as?

754. Who founded the U.S. Army Signal Corps?

755. What two components comprised the method of communication of the U.S. Army Signal Corps?

756. What was General Robert E. Lee's General Order No. 61?

757. Who was the Civil War's only *official* Army photographer?

758. What Union general captured Norfolk, Virginia?

759. For the Confederacy, what was the most important result of the Battle of Seven Pines (Fair Oaks)?

760. What battle changed the course of the war in the East from a maneuver war to a siege war?

761. In *Gone With the Wind*, what was Scarlett O'Hara's father's first name?

762. Who was "Petroleum V. Nasby"?

763. What Pennsylvania regiment dug the long tunnel that resulted in the Battle of the Crater in Petersburg, Virginia?

764. What was the popular name of the 1st Brigade of the 1st Division of the Union 1st Corps?

765. Who was Annie Etheridge?

766. For the purpose of Congressional appointment, how were slaves counted?

767. Who was the model for Tom in the novel *Uncle Tom's Cabin?*

768. What was known as the Pottawatomie Massacre?

769. Who fired the first Union shot from Fort Sumter, South Carolina?

770. Who suggested the army use of the French *tent d'abri,* referred to by U.S. soldiers as the "pup tent"?

771. What unit was known as the Tammany Regiment?

772. How many fifers (fife players) did each Union infantry company have?

773. How many horses were required to pull the Federals' biggest gun?

774. Who was Chairman of the Joint Committee on the Conduct of the War?

775. What type of units used bugles and trumpets to play certain calls?

776. Who were the "butternuts"?

777. To what unit was Oliver Wendell Holmes, Jr. assigned?

778. What was the purpose of infantry company drummers?

779. What Confederate general, at the Battle of Seven Pines (Fair Oaks), rode slowly through enemy fire smoking a cigar?

780. How many Federal gunboats were involved at the Battle of Drewry's Bluff near Richmond, Virginia?

Interior of Fort Sumter during the bombardment

781. Why did Union General O.O. Howard say to Union General Phil Kearney, "We can buy our gloves together"?

782. Why was Confederate General Joseph Johnston's sword so important to him?

783. What was the best time for observation from a balloon?

784. What was the 20th Massachusetts Infantry known as?

785. What was the Union aeronaut's (Professor T.S.C. Lowe) preferred observation altitude from his balloon?

786. At what battle did Lee say, "The enemy is there, and I am going to strike him"?

787. How did General George Pickett rank in his West Point graduation?

788. What was distinctive about Private Joseph L. Pierce of the 14th Connecticut?

789. What type of weapon did most Union and Confederate soldiers use in Pickett's charge at Gettysburg?

790. At the Battle of Gettysburg, what Union general was wounded with a tenpenny nail?

791. What was General William T. Sherman's nickname?

792. Who first hoisted the American flag over the capitol in Richmond after the surrender?

793. How did the ironclad C.S.S. *Virginia* (*Merrimac*) end its career?

794. Under whose administration did Jefferson Davis serve as secretary of war?

795. At what battle did Grant break Lee's line to capture Petersburg?

796. McClellan's Second Corps commander was General Edwin V. Sumner. What was his nickname?

797. After what great battle did Lincoln issue his Emancipation Proclamation?

A bomb-proof in Fort Hell
before Petersburg

798. What was Grant's best subject at West Point?

799. Who was Robert E. Lee's father?

800. Who replaced General McDowell as commander of the Army of the Potomac?

801. About whom was Lincoln talking when he said, "I can't spare this man. He fights."

802. Who was General U.S. Grant's chief of staff?

803. Who was the first soldier in the history of the New World to command an army of 100,000 field soldiers?

804. Who was U.S. Grant's best man at his wedding?

805. Which of General Robert E. Lee's sons was a cavalry officer?

806. Why are there not many signs saying, "Lee slept here" at residences in Virginia?

807. What was Union General Phil Sheridan's horse's name?

808. How many horses were presented as gifts to General U.S. Grant right after the war ended?

809. What was General U.S. Grant's mother's first name?

810. Who served as President U.S. Grant's second vice-president?

811. What was the Stonewall Brigade initially known as?

812. What was the name of Stonewall Jackson's cook and valet?

813. At what battle did the Confederates first scream the famous "rebel yell"?

814. What did Confederate Valley troops call diarrhea?

815. During the war, how many commanders did the Stonewall Brigade have?

816. What famous event occurred in March 1864 between the Stonewall Brigade with a Louisiana brigade against a Georgia brigade with a North Carolina brigade?

817. How many U.S. ships were in active service at the beginning of the war?

818. Approximately how many men served in the Confederate army?

819. How did the South name its armies?

820. How many and what type of members comprised the Committee on the Conduct of the War?

821. What was General U.S. Grant's first Civil War battle?

822. Name four of the five Confederate cities that became principal Federal targets.

823. What was the closest General George McClellan ever got to Richmond?

824. What portion of land between two mountain ranges is a direct route into both the North and South?

825. How many men perished in the Civil War?

826. Name six of the ten most important Southern ports.

827. Within ten, how many prizes did the C.S.S. *Alabama* take in its two years of service?

828. What event did Federal Admiral David Farragut call "one of the happiest moments of my life"?

829. Who did the most to keep Europe neutral during the Civil War?

830. What Confederate official served successively as Confederate attorney general, secretary of war, and secretary of state?

831. At one time, what was the ratio of prisoner exchange for one major-general?

832. What part of the Federal soldier's uniform was the "kepi"?

833. What was Stonewall Jackson's second wife's name?

834. Name one of the subjects that Stonewall Jackson taught at VMI.

835. What Union general became adrift in an observation balloon?

836. What wound did Stonewall Jackson receive at Bull Run (Manassas)?

837. What was the only regiment that poet John Greenlief Whittier ever saw?

838. Who was the free Negro William Tillman?

Sibley tents

839. How old was Alexander Stephens when he was inaugurated as Confederate vice-president?

840. To whom did General U.S. Grant deliver his famous "unconditional and immediate surrender" terms?

841. Where did General U.S. Grant deliver his famous "unconditional and immediate surrender" terms?

842. Whose proposal was it to have Compensated Emancipation?

843. At first, how much was the union Negro soldier paid?

844. How many Negro physicians were commissioned during the war?

845. What state had the second largest number of engagements?

846. Who signed the Civil War Centennial Proclamation?

847. What was the average cost of a musket?

848. What percent of battle casualties was attributed to the artillery?

849. Who signed Robert E. Lee's appointment to the rank of colonel in the U.S. Army?

850. What Union general had the same name as a high official in the Confederacy?

851. Name two of the three former Confederates who held the rank of general in the U.S. Army after the war.

852. How did poet Sidney Lanier die?

853. Who wrote the stanzas of the popular Southern version of "Dixie"?

854. Who commanded the 1st New Mexico Volunteers (Union)?

855. Which Confederate regiment suffered the largest loss in a single battle?

856. How many Confederate regiments went into Pickett's Charge at Gettysburg?

857. How many Confederates received Federal pensions?

858. In what state occurred the third largest number of engagements?

859. At what battle was the Sunken Road, later known as Bloody Lane?

860. At Confederate Andersonville prison, who were the Regulators?

861. How many prisoners successfully escaped from Andersonville prison?

862. Who commanded the Confederate Light Division?

863. Who was the oldest of all Civil War soldiers?

864. What was the second most numerous foreign nationality in the Union army?

865. What caused the Union soldiers to accept blacks as American soldiers?

866. What percent of wounds were attributed to bayonets and sabers?

867. Name one of the most widely read publications in Confederate army camps.

868. What was the all-time favorite song of Civil War troops?

869. Who was known as the Angel of Marye's Heights?

870. How many surgeons did the Union forces have?

871. Who was at the head of the U.S. Medical Department at the beginning of the war?

872. How many medical thermometers were used in all of the Union armies?

873. Who was the final casualty of Civil War prison camps?

874. What drum beat signaled the call to arms?

875. What were "file closers"?

876. What was General McClellan's opinion of Abraham Lincoln?

877. What general was responsible for the Union's first major success of the war?

878. Based on his initials, what was Union General N.P. Banks often called?

879. What was the famous Harrison's Landing Letter?

880. What did Lincoln feel was the proper objective of the Union armies?

881. What percent of white families owned slaves in 1860?

882. What were the South's impoverished whites called?

883. What group organized the first national military draft on the North American continent?

884. How many secretaries of war did Jefferson Davis have?

885. Where was the Confederacy's largest gunpowder manufacturing facility?

886. Who owned and managed Richmond's Tredegar Iron Works?

887. Which member of Jefferson Davis's Cabinet was a Jew?

888. Who said, "Convey to Jeff Davis my personal and official thanks for abolishing cotton and substituting corn and sweet potatoes"?

889. What three ingredients were required to make gunpowder?

890. Who was the most successful of the Confederate humorists?

891. How many blacks served as fighting troops in the Confederacy?

892. What famous war poem was later set to the tune of *O Tannenbaum*?

893. Which Confederate secretary of war lasted longest in office?

894. The surrender of what city caused the Confederacy to be split in two?

895. What Confederate three-star general voluntarily resigned his commission and served as a lieutenant colonel for the remainder of the war?

896. By what method was Vicksburg captured?

897. How many attorneys general did Jefferson Davis have?

898. What two famous battles marked the beginning of the end of the Confederacy?

899. What was Union general Joshua L. Chamberlain's occupation before the war?

900. At what point in Lee's line was the famous Crater explosion in Petersburg, Virginia?

901. What Confederate general led the Beefsteak Raid behind Union lines?

902. In what campaign did more black soldiers participate than any other?

903. What was the only pre-approved battlefield promotion of the war?

904. How long was the siege of Vicksburg?

905. Name the date of the Crater Explosion in Petersburg, Virginia.

906. Who were Shannon's Scouts?

907. Who wrote *The Rise and Fall of the Confederate Government?*

908. What are the provisions of the 15th Amendment to the Constitution?

909. After his capture, Jefferson Davis continued to assert that secession was a constitutional right. What high U.S. official agreed with him?

910. What unique type of military unit was deployed for the first time in history at the Battle of Fredericksburg?

911. What Union general was literally left "standing at the altar" on his first attempt at marriage?

Star of the West, a Federal steamship

912. What was General William T. Sherman's attitude toward newsmen?

913. In *Gone With the Wind,* what was Scarlett O'Hara's mother's first name?

914. Who commanded the Iron Brigade?

915. Before the war, how did the United States Constitution recognize slaves?

916. To what unit did Robert E. Lee belong during the John Brown incident at Harper's Ferry?

917. What was distinctive about the headgear of the members of the Union's Iron Brigade?

918. During Pickett's Charge at Gettysburg, what Confederate general placed his hat on the tip of his sword as he advanced?

919. What position did General George Meade's son hold during the Battle of Gettysburg?

920. For what reason did the U.S. Congress grant fifteen medals of honor to individual soldiers after the Battle of Gettysburg?

921. What position did General William T. Sherman hold before the war?

922. At what time of day did Richmond fall?

923. What kin was Robert E. Lee's wife to Martha Washington?

924. What office did Confederate General Longstreet hold after the war?

925. What year was Jefferson Davis released from prison?

926. For what reason were regiments from the Army of the Potomac sent to New York City in the summer of 1863?

927. What Union general bragged that his headquarters would be "in the saddle"?

928. How was General James Longstreet wounded at the Wilderness?

929. To whom was General Robert E. Lee referring when he said, "Gentlemen, the Army of the Potomac has a head"?

930. Which of General Robert E. Lee's sons was an artilleryman?

931. Of what political persuasion was former General George B. McClellan?

932. Who commanded Confederate troops at the attack of Fort Steadman at Petersburg, Virginia?

933. Who first bought the table General U.S. Grant had used for writing the surrender draft at Appomattox?

934. At what address in Washington did General U.S. Grant live after the war?

935. Who was the first woman in the world to be given a degree as Doctor of Medicine?

936. Who was the only woman member of the Grand Army of the Republic (GAR)?

937. What two states maintained governments in exile in the Confederacy?

938. Name the person who held the following three different Confederate portfolios during the war: attorney general, secretary of war, and secretary of state.

939. To what was Confederate vice-president Alexander Stephens referring when he said, "The mountain labors and brings forth a mouse"?

940. Which side was the first to pass a conscription law?

941. What two Confederate cabinet members held their original positions until the end of the war?

942. Who was General Robert E. Lee's Chief of Artillery?

943. What company produced the most cannon for the Confederacy?

944. Who was the first surgeon general of the Confederate army?

945. Who was called the King of Spades?

A casemate

946. What was the title of the most popular religious tract for the soldiers?

947. What company produced the iron plating for the C.S.S. *Virginia* (*Merrimac*)?

948. What German Union general was director of public schools in St. Louis before the war?

949. Where were the Confederate Naval Rope Works located?

950. What were ships that relied on cotton bales for protection called?

951. Who was known as the Poet Laureate of the Confederacy?

952. Where was the last Confederate Cabinet meeting?

953. What were known as Sherman's neckties?

954. Who was called the Bard of the Stars and Bars?

955. What popular foreign novel gave the nickname "Lee's Miserables" to the ill-clad, ill-fed Confederate soldiers?

956. What previous war gave many of the West Point graduates wartime experience?

957. What insignia was the first to be used to identify an army division?

958. What Union general did General Phil Sheridan relieve of his command after the Battle of Five Forks?

959. Why was the 11th New York outfit called the Fire Zouaves?

960. What was the Union 43rd Ohio Regiment known as?

961. About whom was General William T. Sherman speaking when he said, "He had never read a military book in his life, but he had a genius for strategy"?

962. How did the U.S. Army Signal Corpsmen communicate at night?

963. In what city did Jefferson Davis die?

964. Which of General Robert E. Lee's sons was a military aide to President Jefferson Davis?

965. For what did General U.S. Grant apologize to General Robert E. Lee at the surrender at Appomattox, Virginia?

966. Who bought the table where General Lee sat during the surrender at Appomattox, Virginia?

967. Who served as President U.S. Grant's first vice-president?

968. Who was Franklin Thompson?

969. Who was the only woman reporter at Abraham Lincoln's nomination in 1860?

970. Who designed the Confederate ironclad *Virginia* (*Merrimac*)?

971. What was the purpose of the First Army Division insignia?

972. What Confederate unit did Douglas Southhall Freeman term the "model brigade"?

973. At the beginning, what distinguished Company K, 5th Virginia Regiment in the Stonewall Brigade?

974. What was the age of the oldest drummer boy in the Stonewall Brigade?

975. Why was night signaling by U.S. Army Signal Corpsmen considered perilous?

976. By what other name was the Stonewall Brigade called?

977. Where did the C.S.S. *Shenandoah* furl its Confederate colors?

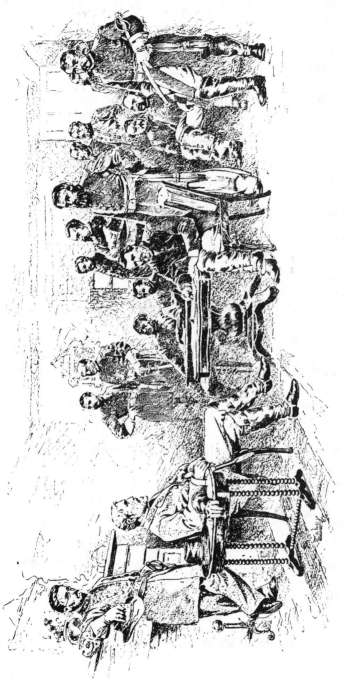

The surrender of Lee to Grant at Appomattox Court House

978. Approximately how many Confederate soldiers died in Federal prisons?

979. What Federal ship was referred to as a "tin can on a shingle"?

980. What did Stonewall Jackson's wives have in common?

981. Why did Union General George McClellan issue an order to give out a half a gill of whiskey each morning to officers and soldiers?

982. What battle caused the Stonewall Brigade to officially cease to exist?

983. Name the ship that carried the 54th Massachusetts Volunteer Regiment to Port Royal, South Carolina.

984. Who organized the 1st South Carolina Volunteer Regiment (Union)?

985. Who said, "The Union could not endure permanently half slave and half free"?

986. What was Abraham Lincoln's second plan for the Negroes?

987. Why was Lincoln called the tortoise president by Abolitionists and Negroes?

988. In what office did Lincoln compose the first draft of the Emancipation Proclamation?

989. Who held the offices of adjutant and inspector general of the Confederate army from 1861 to 1865?

990. In what city did the tune of the Southern version of the song "Dixie" originate?

991. Which regiment suffered the largest loss in a single battle?

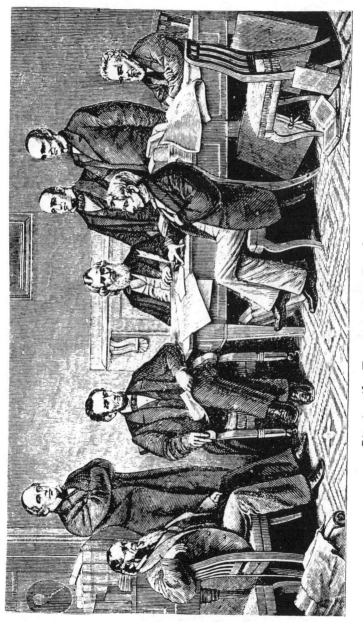

Signing the Emancipation Proclamation

992. How many Confederate regiments were commanded by General Pickett in his famous charge at Gettysburg?

993. At Antietam, what Confederate general saved Lee's forces from apparent disaster?

994. How many years after the war did Jefferson Davis live?

995. How much was paid for the table General Grant had used for writing the surrender draft at Appomattox, Virginia?

996. What was the bloodiest action of the Vicksburg Campaign?

997. Approximately how many Federal soldiers died in Confederate prisons?

998. What nation was the first to introduce in combat an effective warship with heavy iron armor?

999. Who shot and killed Confederate General A.P. Hill?

1000. Name three of the six Andersonville prisoners who were executed (hanged) by fellow inmates.

1001. What age was the oldest Civil War soldier?

ANSWERS

1. North Carolina   (49, p. 76)

2. Ford's   (44, p. 387)

3. General Beauregard   (29v1, p. xxxii)

4. Robert E. Lee   (14, p. xiii)

5. Sixteen (16)   (57, p. 1)

6. Atlanta   (49, p. 597)

7. Johnston's in NC   (49, p. 665)

8. General Beauregard   (29v1, p. xxxii)

9. Clark Gable   (95, p. 151)

10. "Fighting" Joe Hooker   (81, p. 51)

11. Hardtack   (2, p. 13)

12. Antietam (Sharpsburg)   (30v2, p. 387)

13. Mary T. Surratt   (49, p. 694)

14. Jennie Wade   (83, p. 13)

15. Professor T.S.C. Lowe   (14, p. 317)

16. Battle of ironclads *Monitor* and
    Virginia (*Merrimac*)   (49, p. 181)

17. Three (3)   (49, p. 675)

18. Buchanan   (49, p. 4)

19. Virginia   (29, p. 703)

20. General Barnard Bee   (49, p. 98)

21. Battle of Kernstown   (86, p. 206-7)

22. Virginia   (49, p. 117)

23. Northerners who sympathized
    with the South   (56, p. 289)

24. Clara Barton   (44, p. 431)

25. General Custer   (44, p. 436)

26. Grand Army of the Republic   (45, p. 342)

27. "The gallant Pelham"   (14, p. 250)

28. It freed the slaves   (49, p. 696)

29. Tara   (57, p. 1)

30. Confederate General Leonidas Polk (61, Title)

31. Ten year old Johnny Clem   (91, p. 72)

32. A conical, teepee-shaped tent   (2, p. 61-2)

33. Julia Ward Howe   (49, p. 165)

34. General Benjamin Butler   (49, p. 212)

35. Army of Northern VA   (49, p. 219)

36. Confederates   (49, p. 234)

37. General Robert E. Lee   (49, p. 258)

78. General Stonewall Jackson (14, p. 269)

79. Gettysburg (83, p. 22, 28-29)

80. General Sherman (65, p. 11)

81. Shiloh (49, p. 194)

82. Admiral Farragut (49, p. 203)

83. July 4, 1863 (49, p. 379)

84. General U.S. Grant (24, p. 8)

85. Confederates (49, p. 296)

86. General Jeb Stuart (49, p. 226)

87. The Lost Order of Antietam (49, p. 265)

88. Spotsylvania (11v4, p. 170)

89. George B. McClellan (49, p. 563)

90. General Stonewall Jackson (his last words) (29v2, p. 682)

91. General Lew Wallace (88v2, p. 926)

92. General Stonewall Jackson (49, p. 216)

93. Lee's orders prior to the Battle of Antietam (29v2, p. 173)

94. Union General Thomas (49, p. 412)

95. General Sherman (49, p. 565)

96. John Wilkes Booth (3, p. 209)

97. "Dixie" (11v1, p. 553)

118. His left   (11v3, p. 213)

119. His right   (49, p. 676)

120. Major John Pelham   (14, p. 171)

121. Dr. Samuel Mudd   (49, p. 677)

122. Confederates named battles
after towns: (Sharpsburg--town);
Federals named battles after topography:
(Antietam--creek)   (11v2, p. 559)

123. Tarleton   (57, p. 1)

124. Banjoist Joe Sweeney   (32, p. 33-34)

125. His gun   (91, p. 31)

126. General Benjamin Butler   (17, p. 27)

127. SC, MS, FL, AL, GA, LA, TX, VA,
AR, TN, and NC   (49, p. 1075)

128. "Rally behind the Virginians"   (49, p. 98)

129. Pickett's charge at Gettysburg   (63, p. 309)

130. The result of an explosion in
a Union tunnel under a Confederate
fort   (64)

131. Ashley Wilkes   (57, p. 22
                                              et al.)

132. Minie ball   (80, p. 6)

133. Fortress Monroe, VA   (12, title page)

134. Across the street from the
theatre (453 Tenth Street)   (3, p. 218)

135. Eleven (11)	(49, p. 1075)
136. Body lice	(2, p. 80)
137. One (1)	(34, p. 36, 526)
138. Commodore	(34, p. 535)
139. General John C. Pemberton	(27, p. 9, 48)
140. Ten months	(51, p. 1)
141. U.S. Marines	(21, p. 88)
142. General A.P. Hill	(15, p. 11)
143. An engine house	(19v1, p. 45)
144. Episcopalian	(87, App. 111)
145. Petersburg	(19v1, p. 193)
146. General George B. McClellan	(19v2, p. 11)
147. General George B. McClellan	(19v2, p. 11)
148. General J.B. Magruder	(19v2, p. 11)
149. Jewish	(87, App. 111)
150. Lieutenant Colonel Scott Shipp	(19v5, p. 313)
151. Hannibal Hamlin	(19v1, p. 65)
152. Robert E. Lee	(19v1, p. 48)
153. Antietam	(19v3, p. 51)
154. Catholic	(87, App. 111)

176. General Jeb Stuart   (29v2, p. xxiv)

177. General Sherman   (49, p. 483)

178. General Robert E. Lee   (44, p. 446)

179. Pennsylvania   (49, p. 434)

180. Richmond, VA   (37, p. 35)

181. Appomattox Court House   (49, p. 670)

182. Pickett's Charge   (49, p. 377)

183. Virginia Military Institute (VMI)
cadets   (49, p. 501-2)

184. Matthew Brady   (44, pp. 100, 137, 316)

185. Gen. Richard B. Garnett   (69, p. 54)

186. Harriet Beecher Stowe   (46, p. 292)

187. Georgia   (19v6, p. 413)

188. Light Horse Harry Lee (Henry)   (30v1, p. 9, 20)

189. Richmond, VA   (49, p. 462)

190. D.W. Griffith   (46, p. 339)

191. Leslie Howard   (95, p. 141)

192. Lawyer   (46, p. 14)

193. *Uncle Tom's Cabin*   (46, p. 292)

194. Sherman   (44, p. 453)

195. Lincoln's second-term vice-president
and later president of the U.S.   (44, p. 365)

196. Springfield, Illinois   (46, p. 108)

197. Twelve Oaks   (57, p. 16)

198. Olivia De Haviland   (95, p. 141)

199. For hiding in a bombproof
during the Union attack   (22, p. 80, 89)

200. Richmond, VA   (49, p. 161)

201. General Robert E. Lee   (17, p. 45)

202. St. Albans, 1864   (17, p. 66)

203. North Carolina   (17, p. 37)

204. U.S. Grant III and Robert E. Lee IV   (17, p. 23)

205. Abraham Lincoln   (17, p. 57)

206. German   (17, p. 46)

207. VMI cadet casualties at Battle of
New Market   (17, p. 71)

208. Winchester, VA   (17, p. 142)

209. He caught a cold and pneumonia
which caused his death   (17, p. 143)

210. 269   (17, p. 152)

211. The *Hunley*   (17, p. 174)

212. Raphael Semmes   (17, p. 200)

213. John Burns   (17, p. 155)

214. *Deo Vindice* ("God will judge") (17, p. 195)

215. The Springfield rifle (93, p. 34)

216. Winston Churchill (93, p. 39)

217. March 9, 1862 (19v3, p. 120)

218. General Stonewall Jackson (19v3, p. 303)

219. Fredericksburg, VA (19v3, p. 320)

220. Sunday (49, p. 181)

221. On the left side (34, p. 23)

222. Lincoln nicknamed him Tadpole (46, p. 13)

223. *River Queen* (46, p. 24)

224. Abraham Lincoln (46, p. 33)

225. Captain (46, p. 13)

226. Confederate General Joseph Johnston speaking of General Sherman's army (46, p. 16)

227. Laura Keene (46, p. 46)

228. James A. Garfield, former Union general (46, p. 98)

229. General U.S. Grant (46, p. 111)

230. Baltimore, Maryland (46, p. 108)

231. Mahogany (46, p. 110)

232. Easter Sunday after Lincoln's death (46, p. 68)

233. Captain Minie of the French Army (80, p. 6)

234. Charlestown, West Virginia (30v1, p. 402)

235. Sideburns, after General Burnside (75, p. 322)

236. General John B. Hood (49, p. 610)

237. Richmond, Ajax, Lucy Long, and
     Jeff Davis (or Greenbriar) (30, p. 644-6)

238. Jed Hotchkiss (29v1, p. xxvii)

239. Good Friday, April 14, 1865 (49, p. 675)

240. Greensboro, North Carolina (49, p. 674)

241. John H. Reagan (49, p. 683)

242. 1st Maine Heavy Artillery, at
     Petersburg, VA (49, p. 717)

243. Dr. Hunter McGuire (29v1, p. 315)

244. A sutler (50, p. 19)

245. The afternoon (49, p. 670)

246. Montgomery, Alabama (49, p. 76)

247. "Battle Hymn of the Republic" (49, p. 165)

248. William Wallace Lincoln (49, p. 173)

249. Generals Cooper, Lee, Beaure-
     gard, A.S. Johnston, and J.E.
     Johnston (49, p. 113)

250. General Stand Watie (49, p. 192)

251. General George Gordon Meade (81, p. 51)

291. Harrison's Landing, Virginia   (49, p. 246)

292. General John Hunt Morgan   (49, p. 439)

293. Union General John Pope   (49, p. 239)

294. Being replaced by General Burnside   (49, p. 285)

295. Colonel Thomas Higginson   (38, preface)

296. To release Union prisoners   (49, p. 469)

297. Nine (9) percent   (71, p. 29)

298. Shanks   (49, p. 128)

299. John G. Nicolay   (49, p. 121)

300. The mud march   (49, p. 314)

301. Presbyterian   (44, p. 173)

302. The campaign against Petersburg, VA   (65, p. 13)

303. Palm Sunday   (49, p. 670)

304. Lewis Payne (Paine) (Lewis Powell)   (3, p. 222)

305. Four (4)   (65, p. 6)

306. "Our American Cousin"   (44, p. 387)

307. The Union   (49, p. 438)

308. John Tyler   (65, p. 6)

309. Attending St. Paul's Church, Richmond, VA   (49, p. 663-4)

310. The capture of Fort Fisher, NC   (49, p. 625)

311. Marshal Lamon (44, p. 358)

312. Mobile, Alabama (49, p. 673)

313. With a torpedo (49, p. 590)

314. Army of Tennessee (Confederate) and
Army of the Cumberland (Union) (49, p. 610)

315. Amelia Court House, Virginia (49, p. 663)

316. Old Penitentiary Building, Washington,
DC (49, p. 694)

317. 1861 (49, p. 104)

318. One (1) (50, p. 23)

319. Cruelty to Union Prisoners of War (49, p. 693)

320. Old Penitentiary, Washington, DC (44, p. 409)

321. Horace Greeley (49, p. 102)

322. "I beg to present to you, as a
Christmas gift, the City of
Savannah" (49, p. 614)

323. Danville, VA (49, p. 665)

324. Artillerist John Pelham
(Virginia Pelham) (14, p. 250)

325. Port Hudson, LA (49, p. 381)

326. General John C. Breckenridge (49, p. 502)

327. Brevet Lieutenant General (49, p. 470)

328. Battle of Wilson Creek (49, p. 108)

329. Chapel Hill, NC (87, p. 472)

367. General William "Baldy" Smith   (19v6, p. 188)

368. Battle of Chickamauga   (19v5, p. 22)

369. Ambrose Bierce   (19v5, p. 39)

370. Arthur MacArthur, father of General
Douglas MacArthur   (19v5, p. 87)

371. Colonel Elmer Ellsworth   (19v1, p. 171)

372. *Hardee's Tactics*   (19v1, p. 127)

373. The brass Napoleon 12-pounder   (93, p. 34)

374. General Governeur K. Warren   (19v3, p. 409)

375. The Leister family   (19v3, p. 431)

376. Hatteras Island, NC   (43, p. 171)

377. Pensacola, FL   (43, p. 172)

378. Fairfax Court House, Virginia   (43, p. 172)

379. Mary Boykin Chesnut   (53, Title/Author)

380. Dr. John Craven   (12, p. 40)

381. Military authorities   (50, p. 17)

382. Mississippi   (37, p. 392)

383. Georgia   (37, p. 397)

384. General Thomas F. Meagher   (41, Foreword)

385. Virginia   (89, P. 18)

386. Ellen   (47, p. 84)

387. Admiral David G. Farragut (62, p. 108)

388. Vice-president of the United States (62, p. 8)

389. Swiss (31, p. 16)

390. Sinks (31, p. 19)

391. Cape Canaveral, FL (17, p. 13)

392. Excessive fatigue or severe exposure (34, p. 247)

393. *Red Rover* (11v4, p. 361)

394. Baptist (87, App. 111)

395. Secretary William H. Seward (46, p. 111)

396. Four (4) (46, p. 206)

397. Episcopalian (87, App. 111)

398. He was recovering from a wound received the night of Lincoln's assassination (46, p. 111)

399. Fort Jefferson, Dry Tortugas (46, p. 215)

400. Catholic (87, App. 111)

401. Lemon (44, p. 173)

402. Potomac, Rappahannock, York, and James (14, p. 103)

403. Hernia (40v16 No. 1, p. 23)

404. General Hood (49, p. 610)

405. General Nathan Bedford Forrest (49, p. 592)

406. Governor Joe E. Brown (49, p. 597)

407. Pea Ridge, AR (49, p. 180)

408. Island No. 10 (49, p. 196)

409. Seventeen months (49, p. 200)

410. Colonel Henry Pleasants (64, p. 37)

411. Sgt. G.W. Tucker (29v3, p. 679)

412. Shiloh (24, p. 18)

413. General Henry H. Sibley (49, p. 178)

414. Union (49, p. 180)

415. 54th Massachusetts Volunteers (49, p. 359)

416. 18 to 35 (49, p. 200)

417. One aide: Colonel Charles
Marshall (32, p. 15)

418. 5 feet, 8 1/4 inches (49, p. 707)

419. About 10,455 (49, p. 719)

420. Pruning rosebushes (49, p. 34)

421. A horse (49, p. 58)

422. That the war was being fought
to maintain the Union and not
to interfere with slavery (49, p. 101)

423. War elephants (49, p. 166)

424. Forty cents a day and one ration (49, p. 109)

425. Henry W. Bellows, D.D. (4, title page)

426. Twenty-six (44, p. 359)

427. James A. Bailey (Barnum and
Bailey) (50, p. 17)

428. T.S.C. Lowe, balloonist (73, p. 128)

429. Both sides (65, p. 9)

430. General Earl Van Dorn (49, p. 179)

431. He felt it was beyond military
business (49, p. 199)

432. General G.W. Smith (49, p. 219)

433. General Nathaniel Banks (49, p. 217)

434. General P.G.T. Beauregard (49, p. 194)

435. C.S.S. *Arkansas* (49, p. 248)

436. It was the first regiment of free
Negroes (49, p. 272)

437. General Benjamin Butler (49, p. 307)

438. General Braxton Bragg (49, p. 302)

439. Jews (50, p. 29-30)

440. A mammoth Union gun on Morris
Island, SC (49, p. 388)

441. General Braxton Bragg (49, p. 410)

442. Both Lincoln and Davis (49, p. 490)

443. "Fairly won" (49, p. 565)

444. General Franz Sigel (49, p. 502)

445. To vote in state elections (14, p. 304)

446. Generals Grant and Sherman
and Admiral Porter (49, p. 658)

447. Three (3) (49, p. 666)

448. 3 feet, 4 inches (49, p. 707)

449. Three percent of incomes over
$800 (49, p. 104)

450. Kentucky (Lincoln and Davis) (65, p. 6)

451. Between 8,000 and 10,000 (65, p. 12)

452. Two Confederate ironclads being
built in Liverpool, England (49, p. 405)

453. Slightly under 26 years (49, p. 707)

454. Captain R.S. Williams, C.S.A. (94, p. 32-33)

455. Winchester; Guy; The Gray Horse (5, p. 212,
414)

456. William H. Johnson, for desertion (44, p. 111)

457. Generals Polk, Beauregard,
Hardee, Bragg, Hood, Taylor,
Joseph Johnston, and A.E. (40v15 No. 2,
Johnston p. 119)

458. Rainy (44, p. 347)

459. $100 to $130 per month (40v16 No. 1,
p. 18)

460. John La Mountain (35, p. 96)

461. General Curtis (49, p. 179)

481. Fifty-six (56)   (44, p. 364)

482. John Tyler's   (65, p. 6)

483. William Johnson   (44, p. 271)

484. 6th Massachusetts Regiment   (14, p. 72, 83)

485. Suicide   (49, p. 152)

486. Dr. Phineas D. Gurley
(Presbyterian)   (44, p. 399)

487. A devoted friend of Union Western
troops   (44, p. 417)

488. 6 feet, 10 1/2 inches   (49, p. 707)

489. U.S. Navy   (49, p. 666)

490. The capture of President Jefferson
Davis   (49, p. 687)

491. Rice and pork   (49, p. 58)

492. George Washington   (44, p. 271)

493. John C. Fremont   (49, p. 112)

494. Generals Longstreet, Gordon, and
Pendleton   (29v3, p. 745-
748)

495. "Keep up a brave heart" (old
Chinook phrase)   (63, p. 31)

496. Mississippi   (87, p. 455)

497. New Orleans, Louisiana   (44, p. 431)

498. Dr. Charles Leale   (3, p. 213)

499. James Allen   (35, p. 40)

500. The *G.W. Parke Custis*   (72, p. 96n, 169)

501. Slightly less than 170 pounds   (30v1, p. 449)

502. About 10:10 P.M.   (3, p. 206-208)

503. Twenty-three (23)   (3, p. 213)

504. Forty-two dollars   (2, p. 316)

505. Three years   (34, p. 37)

506. *The Village Blacksmith* and *The Horse Fair*   (3, p. 218-219)

507. Every two months   (34, p. 49)

508. Five dollars   (34, p. 546)

509. Gertrude Stein   (15, p. 8)

510. Twelve and one-half (12 1/2) cents   (34, p. 353)

511. Thirteen dollars   (34, p. 353)

512. General John B. Gordon   (15, p. 25)

513. General Jubal A. Early   (15, p. 15)

514. 1907 (18,000 Veterans)   (15, p. 9)

515. One-hundred twenty-four dollars ($124)   (34, p. 358)

516. Forty dollars   (34, p. 398)

517. Judge Richard Parker   (21, p. 91)

518. Rev. Beverly Lacy (11v3, p. 214)

519. Twenty-one dollars (34, p. 546)

520. Sixteen (16) (34, p. 537)

521. One-sixth of his monthly pay (34, p. 531)

522. Four (4) (34, p. 246)

523. Albert Everett, a black servant (15, p. 34)

524. Confederate General Gabriel J. Rains (19v2, p. 48)

525. Union Brigadier General Edwin Sumner (19v2, p. 117)

526. Confederate General Nathan F. "Shanks" Evans (19v2, p. 385)

527. Confederate General William Mahone (19v2, p. 393)

528. General Jefferson C. Davis (19v6, p. 150)

529. Isaac Newton (11v1, p. 741)

530. General William P. Roberts (19v6, p. 342)

531. Jefferson Shields (19v6, p. 448)

532. U.S.S. *Housatonic* (19v5, p. 150)

533. General James Ledlie (19v6, p. 243)

534. Colonel Ely E. Parker, a Seneca Indian (19v5, p. 239)

535. General James Archer (19v3, p. 400)

536. General Edward Ferrero   (19v6, p. 342)

537. Union General David Hunter   (19v5, p. 316)

538. Murdered by a jealous husband   (19v5, p. 413)

539. Over 3000   (19v1, p. 412)

540. Lack of sutler supplies   (50, p. 90)

541. His son was born that morning   (93, p. 31)

542. General Robert Selden Garnett   (43, p. 171)

543. Kensington, CT   (43, p. 388-9)

544. The firing upon the ship *Star of the West*   (43, p. 171)

545. Bailey Thornsberry Brown   (43, p. 182)

546. 1870   (36, p. 390)

547. Chaplain John L. Lenhart   (43, p. 419)

548. Hiram Revels   (36, p. 391)

549. Captain John Quincy Marr   (43, p. 171)

550. Judge John C. Underwood   (36, p. 241)

551. Military District No. 1   (36, p. 390)

552. Horace Greeley   (36, p. 241)

553. General Adelbert Ames (Maine)   (36, p. 392)

554. The long, low street wagons of the Quartermaster Department   (62, p. 37)

555. April 3, 1865   (62, p. 41)

556. The transport ship *Fanny*, which
     carried an observation balloon   (35, p. 96)

557. Presbyterian   (87, App. 111)

558. Jefferson Davis   (17, p. 27)

559. Major M.R. Delaney   (17, p. 31)

560. By kites   (17, p. 31)

561. The skirmish at Bethel, VA   (17, p. 37)

562. Eleven-year-old Grace Bedell   (17, p. 39)

563. George Wills, 49th Pennsylvania   (17, p. 59)

564. Union Brevet Major General
     Galusha Pennypacker   (17, p. 64)

565. Thirty-nine (39)   (17, p. 65)

566. Four dollars   (17, p. 73)

567. It had belonged to George Wash-
     ington   (17, p. 82)

568. Brigadier General William P.
     Roberts (NC)   (17, p. 64)

569. Oliver Wendell Holmes, John M.
     Harlan, William B. Woods, and
     Stanley Matthews   (17, p. 136)

570. Old Abe, an eagle   (17, p. 136)

571. Twenty-nine (29)   (17, p. 142)

572. Edward D. White, Horace H. Lurton,
     and Lucius Q.C. Lamar   (17, p. 136)

573. Simon Bolivar Buckner   (17, p. 143)

574. 546   (17, p. 144)

575. Antonia Ford   (17, p. 150)

576. Charlotte, NC   (17, p. 144-145)

577. In the hairdo of her female agent   (17, p. 146)

578. Richmond, Virginia   (17, p. 146)

579. *The Alligator*   (17, p. 175)

580. General Robert E. Lee   (17, p. 210)

581. Not a single member   (93, p. 19)

582. Leon P. Hopkins--plumber   (46, p. 289)

583. Ninety (90)   (46, p. 311)

584. Chambersburg   (19v5, p. 323)

585. Commander John Worden   (19v3, p. 132)

586. Seventeen (17)   (46, p. vii, Intro.)

587. Lieutenant Catesby Jones   (49, p. 181)

588. A shutter   (46, p. 48)

589. Secretary Edwin M. Stanton   (46, p. 53)

590. Colonel Conger and Lieutenant Baker   (46, p. 189)

591. Six congressmen and six senators   (46, p. 107)

592. Mary Surratt, who was accused of conspiracy for Lincoln's assassination   (46, p. 207)

593. 7:20 p.m. (46, p. 120)

594. Captain Christian Rath (46, p. 206)

595. Old Bob (46, p. 130)

596. The Edward H. Jones (46, p. 115)

597. Louis Weichmann (46, p. 198)

598. Union (46, p. 123)

599. "After all, tomorrow is another
day." (57, p. last)

600. 180,000 (38, Edit.
preface)

601. Governor John Letcher (29v1, p. 4)

602. Milledgeville (60, p. 63)

603. An Italian named Ferrandini (25, p. 14)

604. He scratched his elbows while
thinking (59, p. 60)

605. William Farley, Redmond Burke
and Franklin Stringfellow (29, p. xxviii)

606. Confederacy President Jefferson
Davis (58, p.17)

607. He was a tailor (58, p. 16)

608. General Ambrose Burnside (33, p.26)

609. Father William Corby (33, p. 83)

610. General George B. McClellan (13, p. 4)

611. One (1)   (13, p. 10)

612. 90,000 men   (13, p. 13)

613. Hamilton   (57, p. 5)

614. Civil War journalists and artists   (77, p. 4)

615. Union General Joseph Hooker   (77, p. 194)

616. Three days   (7, p. 256)

617. "The Girl I Left Behind Me"   (7, p. 271)

618. Short staple cotton   (20, p. 29)

619. *Or Life Among the Lowly*   (20, p.47)

620. Seven (7)   (20, p. 168)

621. John Jacob Astor III   (1, p. 22)

622. One (1)   (1, p. 59)

623. Without a fight - the Confederates evacuated   (1, p. 107)

624. The Battle of Seven Pines or the Battle of Fair Oaks   (1, p. 40)

625. General James Longstreet   (78, p. 17)

626. Thirty-eight (38)   (78, p. 24)

627. 17th   (78, p. 25)

628. General W.M. Pendleton   (78, Illustration after p. 146)

629. Arkansas and Texas   (78, p. 175)

630. Fifty-nine (59)   (78, p. 25)

631. Red   (47, p. 1)

632. Bill was dead   (47, p. 491)

633. He approved of it   (47, p. 2)

634. April 3, 1865   (39, p. 1)

635. Brigadier General Josiah Gorgas   (39, p. xiv)

636. The Confederate White House   (39, p. 242)

637. Jefferson Davis   (18, p. 14)

638. She was appointed Postmaster of Richmond   (39, p. 249)

639. By having a certain percentage of its number reenlisting   (39, p. 63)

640. The North   (8, p. 64-65)

641. Hiram Ulysses Grant   (76, p. 12)

642. General Henry Halleck   (76, p. 112)

643. The rifled bullet   (76, p. 209)

644. Three (3)   (76, p. 220)

645. Forty dollars ($40)   (76, p. 276)

646. Secretary of war   (76, p. 290)

647. Governor Andrew Curtin   (16, p. 270, 414)

648. Sarah Emma Edmonds   (16, p. 48)

649. Mary A. (Mother) Bickerdyke   (16, p. 231)

650. Brierfield   (26, p. 48)

651. Eleven (11) states seceded; two
(2) states were only claimed   (26, p. 41)

652. No one; there was no Department
of Agriculture   (26, p. 51)

653. Five-cent   (26, p. 52)

654. Six (6)   (26, p. 52)

655. Russia   (26, p. 79)

656. General P.G.T. Beauregard   (29v1, p. 3)

657. General Robert S. Garnett   (29v1, p. 37)

658. On a train bound north to see his
family   (6, p. 112)

659. Union General Phil Kearney   (6, p. 58)

660. By a drummer   (9, p. 25)

661. Ninety (90) days   (9, p. 25)

662. Senator John J. Crittenden   (9, p. 41)

663. Weights were tied to their tails   (9, p. 48)

664. The Sharps rifles   (9, p. 4)

665. The brigade   (69, p. 6)

666. Virginia's First Brigade   (63, p. vi)

667. Admiral David D. Porter   (69, p. 19)

668. "Our second War of Independence"   (69, p. 49)

669. A Federal cannon shell clipped off the tail of his horse (69, p. 94)

670. Approximately 17,000 (70, p. 7)

671. Eleven (11) (70, p. 7)

672. Over 2,000,000 (70, p. 7)

673. For large rivers (Army of the Potomac) (70, p. 9)

674. Battle of Wilson's Creek, near Springfield, Missouri (70, p. 12)

675. The Balls Bluff Disaster in Virginia (70, p. 12)

676. Civil War: 7 to 1 (Korean War: 50 to 1) (70, p. 60)

677. General Judson Kilpatrick (42, photo p. 53)

678. Professor Thaddeus S.C. Lowe (90, p. 126)

679. Eleanor Junkin (90, p. 109)

680. A former Prussian Dragoon who served with Jeb Stuart (90, p. 268)

681. John A. Andrew (67, p. 8)

682. Robert Gould Shaw (67, p. 9)

683. Frederick Douglass (67, p. 11)

684. 182,000 (67, p. 35)

685. William A. Jackson (67, p. 81)

686. Near Fortress Monroe, VA (67, p. 58)

687. Franklin Buchanan   (66, p. 8)

688. One (1)   (66, p. 9)

689. Eleven (11)   (66, p. 12)

690. Seven (7)   (66, p. 2)

691. Vicksburg   (66, p. 14)

692. Union prison Camp Douglas, IL.   (66, p. 59)

693. Virginia   (66, p. 69)

694. Battle of Antietam (Sharpsburg),
Maryland   (82, p. 1)

695. The Dunkard Church   (82, p. 1)

696. Clara Barton   (82, p. 49-50)

697. Prisoners who robbed, murdered,
and terrorized other prisoners   (31, p. 63)

698. The Light Division   (68, p. 63)

699. Richmond, VA

          (68, p. 321)

700. Sweet Water Creek   (31, p. 2)

701. In Roman numerals, consecutively   (71, p. 24)

702. Charles C. Hay - Age 11   (71, p. 27)

703. The 9th Wisconsin   (71, p. 27)

704. General Stand Watie   (71, p. 29)

705. New army shoes   (71, p. 43)

706. It authorized the President to use escaped slaves in the Union armies (71, p. 30-31)

707. A homemade shelter (71, p. 46)

708. 18 inches (71, p. 57)

709. About 2 1/2 miles per hour (71, p. 61)

710. He stole from nearby farms (71, p. 73)

711. *Harper's Weekly* - Frank Leslie's Illustrated Newspaper (71, p. 82)

712. Because of its overwhelming gambling (71, p. 95)

713. Letter-writing (71, p. 104)

714. 2600 (71, p. 155)

715. Disrespect for authority (71, p. 124)

716. $100 a month (71, p. 174)

717. The U.S. Supreme Court Building (71, p. 213)

718. Sixty (60) rounds (71, p. 214-215)

719. A battle wound (71, p. 216)

720. Union General Irvin McDowell (92, p. 19)

721. Burn (92, p. 182, 195)

722. General Henry W. Halleck (92, p. 140)

723. He was violently opposed to it (92, p. 170)

724. "Slow" (92, p. 177)

725. Forty-two (42) (in 1864) (92, p. 310)

726. Congress could not agree on the extent of its authority (10, p. 10)

727. 150 (10, p. 11)

728. Four (4) (10, p. 14)

729. President Jefferson Davis (10, p. 16)

730. Richmond's Tredegar Iron Works (10, p. 21)

731. Small paper notes issued by the Confederate Treasury (10, p. 33)

732. Kanawha (10, p. 75)

733. Three (NC, SC, VA) (10, p. 152)

734. It deferred from service any planter or overseer on plantations with more than 20 slaves (10, p. 80)

735. President Jefferson Davis (10, p. 15)

736. These were Union artillerymen's meal times (27, p. 45)

737. An oak tree (27, p. 55)

738. *Sic Semper Tyrannis* ("Thus always to tyrants") (22, p. 116)

739. *Sic Semper Tyrannis* ("Thus always to tyrants") (22, p. 116)

740. Sergeant Major (22, p. 120)

741. 258   (23, p. 196-197)

742. Uncle Billy   (60, p. 45, 51)

743. Henry Clay Work   (60, p. 75)

744. Captain Thomas Jordan   (25, p. 24)

745. The 12th Wisconsin Volunteer Infantry   (59, p. 23)

746. Eight (8)   (60, p. 13)

747. The 21st Illinois Volunteers   (59, p. 46)

748. He accused Davis of planning Lincoln's assassination   (58, p. 20)

749. Mrs. Lincoln refused to yield possession of the White House   (58, p. 17)

750. To Macon, Georgia   (58, p. 22)

751. Former Union General Oliver O. Howard   (58, p. 51)

752. A crown of thorns woven by the Pope himself   (58, p. 23)

753. "Confederate grey"   (58, p. 57)

754. Colonel Albert J. Myer, ex-New York physician   (33, p. 42)

755. Wigwag flags and telegraph wires   (33, p. 42, 46)

756. It announced the death of General T.J. (Stonewall) Jackson   (33, p. 161)

757. Captain Andrew J. Russell   (33, p. 162)

758. General John Wool (13, p. 5)

759. The wounding of General Joseph Johnston, resulting in Robert E. Lee becoming Field Commander (13, p. 9)

760. The Battle of Cold Harbor, VA (13, p. 34)

761. Gerald (57, p. 15)

762. Pseudonym for David R. Locke, one of Lincoln's favorite humorists (77, p. 333)

763. The 48th (miners) (7, p. 223)

764. The Iron Brigade (7, p. 271)

765. A female member of the 3rd Michigan Regiment (7, p. 197-198)

766. Each slave was three-fifths of a person (20, p. 30)

767. Escaped slave Josiah Henson (20, p. 46)

768. John Brown's killing of five pro-slavery men at Pottawatomie Creek, Kansas (20, p. 71)

769. Captain (later General) Abner Doubleday (20, p. 147)

770. General George B. McClellan (1, p. 14)

771. The 42nd New York Infantry (1, p. 44)

772. One (1) (1, p. 59)

773. Up to 100 (1, p. 105)

774. Ohio Senator Benjamin Franklin
Wade   (1, p. 65)

775. Cavalry and artillery units   (1, p. 60-61)

776. Confederate soldiers   (78, p. 24)

777. 20th Massachusetts Infantry   (1, p. 38)

778. To play calls that summoned to
meals, drills, inspections, etc.   (1, p. 59)

779. General D.H. Hill (to encourage
his troops)   (1, p. 138)

780. Five (5)   (1, p. 127-
                                           128)

781. Each had lost the opposite arm   (1, p. 161)

782. It was first used by his father
in the Revolutionary War   (1, p. 155-
                                           157)

783. Just before dawn   (1, p. 151)

784. The Harvard Regiment   (1, p. 42)

785. 300 feet (15 mile view)   (1, p. 148

786. Battle of Gettysburg   (78, p. 20)

787. Last   (78, p. 25)

788. He was the only Chinese in the
Army of the Potomac   (78, p. 56)

789. The rifled musket   (78, p. 175)

790. General Winfield Scott Hancock   (78, p. 233)

791. Cump - short for Tecumseh   (47, p. 26)

792. Lieutenant De Peyster, 13th N.Y.
     Artillery   (39, Above p.
                                              199)

793. It was burned by the Confed-
     erates just before Richmond
     surrendered   (39, p. 167)

794. Franklin Pierce's   (18, Foreword,
                                              p. 16)

795. Battle of Five Forks, Virginia   (8, p. 17)

796. Bull of the Woods   (8, p. 201)

797. The Battle of Antietam (Sharps-
     burg)   (8, p. 88)

798. Mathematics   (76, p. 17)

799. Light Horse Harry Lee (Henry)   (76, pp. 6-7)

800. General George McClellan   (76, p. 104)

801. General U.S. Grant   (76, p. 122)

802. John A. Rawlings   (76, p. 108)

803. General George B. McClellan   (76, p. 124)

804. General James Longstreet   (76, p. 43)

805. Rooney   (76, p. 220)

806. He almost always lived in his tent   (76, p. 239)

807. Rienzi   (76, p. 245)

808. Fourteen (14)   (76, p. 284)

809. Hannah   (76, p. 284)

810. Henry Wilson   (76, p. 320)

811. Virginia's First Brigade   (69, p. vi)

812. Jim Lewis   (69, p. 14)

813. At First Manassas (Bull Run)   (69, p. 42)

814. "The Virginia quick-steps"   (69, p. 53)

815. Seven (7)   (69, p. 146-147)

816. The most famous snowball fight in the history of the war   (69, p. 217)

817. Forty-two (42)   (70, p. 7)

818. One million (1,000,000)   (70, p. 7)

819. By large areas of land (Army of Northern Virginia)   (70, p. 9)

820. Seven U.S. Congressmen   (70, p. 12)

821. He suffered a defeat at Belmont, Missouri   (70, p. 13)

822. Richmond, New Orleans, Vicksburg, Chattanooga and Atlanta   (70, p. 13)

823. Seven Pines, VA   (70, p. 17)

824. The Shenandoah Valley   (70, p. 17)

825. Over 618,000   (70, p. 35)

826. Norfolk, New Bern, Wilmington, Beaufort, Charleston, Savannah, Pensacola, Mobile, New Orleans and Galveston   (70, p. 37)

827. Sixty-two (62)   (70, p. 39)

828. The end of the C.S.S. *Arkansas*   (70, p. 40)

829. American Minister to England
Charles Francis Adams   (70, p. 44)

830. Judah P. Benjamin   (70, p. 43)

831. Forty (40) privates   (70, p. 45)

832. A cap that slanted toward the
front   (70, p. 58)

833. Mary Anna Morrison   (90, p. 109)

834. Artillery and Natural Philosophy   (90, p. 108)

835. General Fitz John Porter   (90, p. 126)

836. The longest finger of his left hand
was broken   (90, p. 110)

837. The 54th Massachusetts (Negro)   (67, p. 11)

838. Tillman sailed on the *S.J. Waring*
as a steward and returned as
the captain   (67, p. 32)

839. Forty-nine (49)   (67, p. 42)

840. To Confederate General Simon
Buckner   (67, p. 74)

841. At Fort Donelson, Tennessee   (67, p. 74)

842. Abraham Lincoln   (67, p. 137)

843. $10 minus $3 for clothing   (67, p. 200)

844. Eight (8)   (67, p. 203)

845. Tennessee (66, p. 69)

846. Dwight D. Eisenhower (66, inside back cover)

847. Thirteen (13) dollars (66, p. 16)

848. Twenty (20) percent (66, p. 54)

849. Abraham Lincoln (66, p. 7)

850. General Jefferson Davis (66, p. 7)

851. Matthew C. Butler, Fitzhugh Lee and Joe Wheeler (66, p. 8)

852. From tuberculosis contracted while in a Union prison (66, p. 9)

853. New England poet Albert Pike (66, p. 9)

854. The famous Kit Carson (66, p. 10)

855. The 26th NC Infantry - Gettysburg (66, p. 13)

856. Forty-six (46) (66, p. 13)

857. Two (2) (66, p. 15)

858. Missouri (66, p. 69)

859. Battle of Antietam (82, p. 36-37)

860. Prison inmates organized to maintain order within the stockade (31, p. 71)

861. 329 (31, p. 49)

862. General A.P. Hill (68, p. 63)

879. A letter from General McClellan giving political advice to President Lincoln (92, p. 133)

880. The destruction of the Confederate armies and not the occupation of Southern Territories (92, p. 7, 234, 253)

881. About 25 percent (10, p. 8)

882. Peckerwoods, or poor whites (10, p. 8)

883. The Confederate Congress (10, p. 13)

884. Six (6) (10, p. 14)

885. Augusta, Georgia (10, p. 20)

886. General Joseph R. Anderson (10, p. 20)

887. Judah Benjamin (10, p. 15)

888. Union General William T. Sherman (10, p. 29-30)

889. Charcoal, sulfur and niter (Saltpeter) (10, p. 19)

890. "Bill Arp" (Charles Henry Smith) (10, p. 51)

891. None (10, p. 166-167)

892. *Maryland! My Maryland* (10, p. 49)

893. James A. Seddon (10, p. 15)

894. Vicksburg, Mississippi (27, p. 1)

895. Lieutenant Ceneral John C. Pemberton   (27, p. 54)

896. By siege   (27, p. 33-41)

897. Five (5)   (10, p. 14)

898. Gettysburg and Vicksburg   (27, p. 52-53)

899. Professor of Theology at Bowdoin College, Maine   (22, p. 51)

900. At Elliott's Salient   (22, p. 70-75)

901. General Wade Hampton   (22, p. 115)

902. The besieging of Petersburg   (22, p. 117)

903. Grant's promotion of Joshua L. Chamberlain to Brigadier General   (22, p. 51)

904. Forty-seven (47) days   (22, p. 53)

905. July 30, 1864   (22, p. 76)

906. A 30-man Confederate outfit that harassed Sherman's army as it crossed Georgia   (60, p. 55)

907. Jefferson Davis   (58, p. 24)

908. It eliminated race, color or previous condition of servitude as legal barriers to voting   (58, p. 99)

909. The Chief Justice of the Supreme Court   (58, p. 20)

910. The U.S. Army Signal Corps   (33, p. 42)

911. General Ambrose Burnside   (33, p. 27)

912. He was a relentless enemy of newsmen (77, p. 176-182)

913. Ellen (57, p. 5)

914. General Soloman J. Meredith (7, p. 46-47)

915. As chattel property (20, p. 29)

916. 2nd U.S. Cavalry (20, p. 88)

917. They wore black hats (7, p. 216, 223)

918. General Lew Armistead (78, p. 180)

919. He was his father's aide (78, p. 249)

920. For capturing enemy flags (78, p. 270)

921. He was head of the Louisiana State Seminary of Learning and Military Academy (later Louisiana State University (47, p. 1)

922. 8:15 AM (39, p. 1)

923. ∧GREAT Granddaughter (39, p. 5)

924. He was appointed U.S. Minister to Turkey (39, p. 246)

925. 1867 (18, p. 12)

926. To quell one of the country's worst riots, caused by the Civil War Draft Law (8, p. 58-59)

927. General John Pope (76, p. 136)

928. He was hit by a volley from his
own men (76, p. 196)

929. General U.S. Grant (76, p. 198)

930. Rob (76, p. 220)

931. Democratic (76, p. 228)

932. General John B. Gordon (76, p. 244)

933. Union General Phil Sheridan (76, p. 276)

934. 205 "I" Street, N.W. (76, p. 285)

935. Dr. Elizabeth Blackwell (16, p. 54)

936. Sarah Emma Edmonds (16, p. 397)

937. Kentucky and Missouri (26, p. 308,
notes)

938. Judah P. Benjamin (26, p. 52)

939. The Confederate Congress (26, p. 55)

940. The Confederates (26, p. 85)

941. Steven Mallory and John Reagon (26, p. 52)

942. General William N. Pendleton (26, p. 102)

943. The Tredegar Iron Works, Richmond, Virginia (26, p. 136)

944. Samuel Preston Moore (26, p. 98)

945. General Robert E. Lee (26, p. 97)

946. *A Mother's Parting Words to Her
Soldier Boy* (26, p. 101)

965. For his (Grant's) sloppy dress
and appearance   (76, p. 274)

966. General Edward Ord   (76, p. 276)

967. Schuyler Colfax   (76, p. 305)

968. A lady who served as a soldier in
the Union army   (16, p. 48)

969. Mary Livermore   (16, p. 37)

970. Commander John Mercer Brooke   (26, p. 174)

971. To identify stragglers from a certain
division   (6, p. 58)

972. Stonewall Jackson's Brigade   (69, p. VII)

973. Its uniforms were exact replicas
of George Washington's Revo-
lutionary Army uniforms   (69, p. 19)

974. Fifty-seven (57) - Private David
Scantlon   (69, p. 14)

975. Wigwagging with flaming torches
made the men easy sharp-
shooter targets   (33, p. 45)

976. Stonewall's Band; Jackson's Foot
Cavalry; The Men of Manassas   (69, p. vii)

977. In Liverpool, England   (70, p. 39)

978. Approximately 26,000   (70, p. 47)

979. The U.S.S. *Monitor*   (70, p. 40)

980. They both were minister's daugh-
ters   (90, p. 109)

999. Corporal John W. Mauck, 138th
  Pennsylvania   (68, p. 318)

1000. Sullivan, Collins, Delaney, Curtis, Sarsfield, and A. Munn   (31, p. 71)

1001. Eighty (80)   (71, p. 26)

REFERENCES

1. Bailey, Ronald H., *Forward to Richmond*, Alexandria, Va., Time-Life Books, 1983.

2. Billings, John D., *Hardtack and Coffee*, Boston, George M. Smith & Company, 1888.

3. Bishop, Jim, *The Day Lincoln Was Shot*, N.Y., Harper & Bros., 1955.

4. Brockett, L.P. and Vaughan, Mary C., *Woman's Work in the Civil War*, Philadelphia, Ziegler, McCurdy and Co., 1987.

5. Burr, Frank and Hinton, Richard J., *The Life of General Philip H. Sheridan*, Providence, R.I., J.A. and R.A. Reid, Publishers, 1888.

6. Catton, Bruce, *America Goes to War*, Middletown, Conn., Wesleyan University Press, 1958.

7. Catton, Bruce, *Glory Road*, Garden City, N.Y., Doubleday & Company, Inc., 1952.

8. Catton, Bruce, *Reflections on the Civil War*, Garden City, N.Y., Doubleday & Company, Inc., 1981.

9. Catton, Bruce, *This Hallowed Ground*, Garden City, N.Y., Doubleday Company, Inc., 1956.

10. Channing, Steven A., *Confederate Ordeal*, Alexandria, Virginia, Time-Life Books, 1984.

11. Century Magazine, *Battles and Leaders of the Civil War*, 4 volumes, New York-London, Thomas Yoseloff, 1956.

12. Craven, John J., *Prison Life of Jefferson Davis*, N.Y., G.W. Dillingham Co., 1905.

13. Cullen, Joseph P., *Richmond National Battlefield Park*, Washington, D.C., National Park Service Historical Handbook Series No. 33, 1961.

14. Commager, Henry S., *The Blue and The Gray*, New York, New American Library, A Mentor Book, 1973.

15. Dabney, Virginius, *The Last Review*, Chapel Hill, N.C., Algonquin Books, 1984.

16. Dannett, Sylvia G.L., *Noble Women of the North*, New York/London, Thomas Yoseloff, 1959.

17. Davis, Burke, *Our Incredible Civil War*, New York, Holt, Rinehart and Winston, 1966.

18. Davis, Jefferson, *The Rise and Fall of the Confederate Government*, New York, N.Y., Collier Books, 1961

19. Davis, William C., Editor, *The Image of War: 1861-1865*, Vols. I, II, III, V, VI, Garden City, N.Y., Doubleday & Co., 1981-1984.

20. Davis, William C., *Brother Against Brother--The War Begins*, Alexandria, Va., Time-Life Books, 1983.

21. Davis, William C., *The Civil War--Brother Against Brother*, New York, Holt, Rinehart & Winston, 1966.

22. Davis, William C., *Death in the Trenches*, Alexandria, Va., Time-Life Books, 1986.

23. Davis, William C., *The Battle of New Market*, Garden City, N.Y., Doubleday & Company, Inc., 1975.

24. Dillahunty, Albert, *Shiloh*, Washington, D.C., National Park Service Historical Handbook, Series No. 10, 1961 Reprint.

25. Editors, Time-Life Books, *Spies, Scouts and Raiders*, Alexandria, Va., Time-Life Books, 1985.

26. Eaton, Clement, *A History of the Southern Confederacy*, New York, The MacMillan Co., 1954

27. Everhart, William C., *Vicksburg*, Washington, D.C., National Park Service Historical Handbook Series 21, 1961.

28. Fox, William F., *Regimental Losses in the American Civil War*, Albany, Albany Publishing Co., 1889.

29. Freeman, Douglas S., *Lee's Lieutenants*, 3 volumes, New York, Charles Scribners Sons, 1942, 1943, 1944.

30. Freeman, Douglas S., *R.E. Lee*, 4 volumes, New York, Charles Scribners Sons, 1946.

31. Futch, Ovid L., *History of Andersonville Prison*, University of Florida Press, Gainesville, Florida, 1968.

32. Gills, Mary Louise, *It Happened at Appomattox*, Richmond, The Dietz Press, 1948.

33. Goolrick, William K., *Rebels Resurgent*, Va., Time-Life Books, 1985.

34. Government Printing Office, *Revised U.S. Army Regulations of 1861*, Washington, 1863.

35. Haydon, F. Stansburg, *Aeronautics in the Union and Confederate Armies*, Baltimore, Johns Hopkins Press, 1941.

36. Henry, Robert Selph, *The Story of Reconstruction* (Reprint), Gloucester, Mass., Peter Smith, 1963.

37. Henry, Robert Selph, *The Story of the Confederacy*, N.Y., Grosset & Dunlap, 1936.

38. Higginson, Thomas W., *Army Life in a Black Regiment*, Williamston, Mass., Corner House Publishers, 197-.

39. Hoehling, A.A. and Hoehling, Mary, *The Day Richmond Died*, San Diego/New York, A.S. Barnes & Co., Inc., 1981.

40. Hubbell, John T., *Civil War History: A Journal of the Middle Period*, Vols. XII, No. 2; XV, No. 2; XVI, No. 1, Kent, Ohio, Kent State University Press, 1969.

41. Jones, Paul, *The Irish Brigade*, Washington-New York, Robt. B. Luce, Inc., 1969.

42. Jones, Virgil Carrington, *Eight Hours Before Richmond*, New York, Henry Holt & Co, 1957.

43. Kane, Joseph Nathan, *Famous First Facts*, 4th Edition, H.W. Wilson Co., New York, 1981.

44. Leech, Margaret, *Reveille in Washington, 1860-1865*, New York, Harper & Bros., 1941.

45. Levey, Judith S. and Greenhall, Agnes, Eds., *The Concise Columbia Encyclopedia*, New York, Columbia University Press, 1983.

46. Lewis, Lloyd, *Myths After Lincoln*, New York, The Press of the Readers Club, 1941.

47. Lewis, Lloyd, *Sherman-Fighting Prophet*, New York, Harcourt, Brace and Company, 1932.

48. Lewis, Mort Reis, *The Civil War Horse*, Richmond, Official Publication No. 10, Richmond Civil War Centennial Committee, ND.

49. Long, E.B., *The Civil War Day By Day*, Garden City, N.Y., Doubleday & Co., 1971.

50. Lord, Francis A., *Civil War Sutlers and Their Wares*, Cranbury, N.J., Thomas Yoseloff, Publishers, 1969.

51. Lykes, Richard Wayne, *Campaign for Petersburg*, Washington, D.C., National Park Services, U.S. Dept. of the Interior, 1970.

52. Manucy, Albert, *Artillery Through the Ages*, Washington, D.C., U.S. Government Printing Office, 1949.

53. Martin, Isabella and Avary, Myrta, *A Diary for Dixie*, New York, D. Appleton & Co., 1905.

54. McCarthy, Carleton, *Soldier Life in the Army of Northern Virginia*, Richmond, Carleton McCarthy & Co., 1882.

55. Meredith, Roy, Ed., McElroy, John, *This Was Andersonville*, New York, Bonanza Books, MCMLVII.

56. Mish, Frederick C., Editor, *Webster's Ninth New Collegiate Dictionary*, Springfield, Mass., Merriam-Webster, Inc., 1983.

57. Mitchell, Margaret, *Gone With the Wind*, New York, The MacMillan Co., 1936.

58. Murphy, Richard W., *The Nation Reunited*, Alexandria, Va., Time-Life Books, 1987.

59. Nevin, David, *The Road to Shiloh*, Alexandria, Va., Time-Life Books, 1983.

60. Nevin, David, *Sherman's March*, Alexandria, Va., Time-Life Books, 1986.

61. Parks, Joseph H., *General Leonidas Polk, CSA, The Fighting Bishop*, Baton Rouge, Louisiana State University Press, 1962.

62. Patrick, Rembert W., *The Fall of Richmond*, Baton Rouge, Louisiana State University Press, 1960.

63. Pickett, LaSalle Corbett, *Pickett...And His Men*, Atlanta, The Foote and Davies Co., 1900.

64. Pleasants, Henry J., *The Tragedy of the Crater*, Washington, Eastern National Park and Monument Assn., 1975 Reprint.

65. Price, William H., *Civil War Centennial Handbook*, Arlington, Virginia, Prince Lithograph Co., 1961.

66. Price, William H., *Civil War Handbook*, Fairfax, Va., Prince Lithograph Co., 1961.

67. Quarles, Benjamin, *The Negro in the Civil War*, Boston, Mass., Little, Brown and Co., 1953.

68. Robertson, James I. Jr., *General A.P. Hill*, New York, Random House, 1987.

69. Robertson, James I. Jr., *The Stonewall Brigade*, Baton Rouge and London, Louisiana State University Press, 1963.

70. Robertson, James I., Jr., *The Civil War*, Washington, D.C., U.S. Civil War Centennial Commission, 1963.

71. Robertson, James I., Jr., *Soldiers Blue and Gray*, Columbia, S.C., University of South Carolina Press, 1988.

72. Rolt, L.T.C., *The Aeronauts*, New York, Walker & Co., 1966.

73. Sandburg, Carl, *Storm Over the Land*, New York, Harcourt, Brace and World, Inc., 1939.

74. Sherman, William T., *Memoirs of General William T. Sherman by Himself*, Vol. II, N.Y., D. Appleton and Co., 1875.

75. Shipley, Joseph H., *Dictionary of Word Origins*, New York, Philosophical Library, Inc., MCMXLV.

76. Smith, Gene, *Lee and Grant*, New York, McGraw-Hill, 1984.

77. Starr, Louis M., *Bohemian Brigade*, New York, Alfred A. Knopf, 1954.

78. Stewart, George, R., *Pickett's Charge*, Boston, Houghton-Mifflin Co., 1959.

79. Stine, J.H., *History of the Army of the Potomac*, Philadelphia, 1982.

80. Stonewall Jackson Memorial, *Facts About the Civil War*, Lexington, Va., ND.

81. Symonds, Craig L., *A Battlefield Atlas of the Civil War*, Annapolis, Md., The Nautical and Aviation Publishing Co. of America, 1983.

82. Tilberg, Frederick, *Antietam*, Washington, D.C., National Park Service Historical Handbook Series 31, 1961.

83. Tilberg, Frederick, *Gettysburg National Military Park*, Washington, National Park Service Historical Handbook Series, No. 9, 1961 Reprint.

84. Time-Life Books, Editors, *Spies, Scouts and Raiders*, Alexandria, Va., Time-Life Books, 1985.

85. U.S. Sanitary Commission, *Ages of U.S. Volunteer Soldiers*, New York, 1866.

86. Vandiver, Frank, *Mighty Stonewall*, New York, McGraw-Hill Book Co., 1957.

87. Wakelyn, Jon L., *Biographical Dictionary of the Confederacy*, Westport, Conn., Greenwood Press, 1977.

88. Wallace, Lew, *Lew Wallace, An Autobiography*, 2 vols., New York, Harper & Bros., 1906.

89. Wesley, Charles H. and Romero, Patricia W., *Negro Americans*, New York, Publishers Co., Inc., 1970.

90. Wheeler, Richard, *Sword Over Richmond*, New York, Harper & Row Publishers, 1986.

91. Wiley, Bell I., *The Common Soldier in the Civil War*, New York, Charles Scribner's Sons, 1973.

92. Williams, T. Harry, *Lincoln and His Generals*, New York, Alfred A. Knopf, 1952.

93. Williams, T. Harry, *The Selected Essays of T. Harry Williams*, Louisiana State University Press, Baton Rouge and London, 1983.

94. Wise, Jennings, *Long Arm of Lee*, 2 vols., Lynchburg, Va., J.P. Bell Co., Inc., 1915.

95. Zinman, David, *50 Classic Motion Pictures*, New York, Bonanza Books, 1970.